"I love the winning, I can take the losing, but most of all I love to play the game."

GAMES COMPANIES PLAY

The Job Hunter's Guide to

Playing Smart & Winning Big in

the High-Stakes Hiring Game

by Dr. Pierre Mornell

Designed by Kit Hinrichs

Illustrations by Regan Dunnick

Ten Speed Press

BERKELEY   TORONTO

A Kirsty Melville Book

Ten Speed Press
P.O. Box 7123
Berkeley, California 94707
www.tenspeed.com

Distributed in Australia by Simon and Schuster Australia, in Canada by Ten Speed Press Canada, in New Zealand by Southern Publishers Group, in South Africa by Real Books, in Southeast Asia by Berkeley Books, and in the United Kingdom and Europe by Airlift Books.

Cover and interior design by Kit Hinrichs/Pentagram

Library of Congress Cataloging-in-Publishing Data

Mornell, Pierre.

Games companies play : the job hunter's guide to playing smart and winning big in the high-stakes hiring game / Pierre Mornell ; designed by Kit Hinrichs ; illustrations by Regan Dunnick ; edited by Doris Ober

p.   cm.

Includes bibliographical references and index.

ISBN 1-58008-183-5 (Cloth)

1. Job hunting.   I. Hinrichs, Kit.   II. Dunnick, Regan.   III. Title.
HF5382.7 .M686 2000
650.14—dc21   00-026736

First printing, 2000
Printed in Hong Kong
1 2 3 4 5 6 7 8 9 10 - 04 03 02 01 00

For Sascha, Sara, Mara, and Eric

Contents

Part 3: Strategies After the Interview **127**

Conclusion **155**

Summary Chart for Games Companies Play **161**

End Games **173**

The Job Hunter's Internet **187**

Resource Books **189**

Notes **191**

Acknowledgments **195**

About the Author, Designer, and Illustrator **196**

Index **199**

Author's Note ☞ *Scattered throughout the book are sixteen summary charts of different personality types. These charts are to help you relate your personality to the prospective job situation.*

Here are my three suggestions for reading the charts:

1. *Choose the personality types that describe you best.*
2. *Check off the strengths and weaknesses that you feel apply to you.*
3. *Select those strengths and weaknesses that best relate to the position for which you will interview.*

These charts are the starting point for a discussion—your thoughts are what counts. With a better understanding of your talents and shortcomings, you'll be better equipped to play up the former—and account for the latter—in most interviews.

A Cautionary Tale

nce upon a time, a highly successful executive was hit by a bus, and she died. She was met at the pearly gates by St. Peter himself. "Welcome to Heaven," said St. Peter. "Before you get settled in though, it seems we have a problem. Strangely enough, we've never once had an executive make it this far, and we're not really sure this is where you belong. What we're going to do is let you have a day in Hell and a day in Heaven. Then you can choose where you want to spend your eternity."

"Actually," said the woman, "I think I'd prefer to stay in Heaven."

"Sorry, we have rules...," said St. Peter, and with that, he put the executive in an elevator, and it went down, down, down to Hell.

The doors opened, and the executive stepped out onto the putting green of a beautiful golf course. In the distance was a country club, and there to greet her were her business associates, friends, and colleagues, all dressed in evening clothes and cheering for her. They ran up and kissed her on both cheeks, and they talked about old times. They played a great round of golf and went to the country club for dinner and dancing at night, where she enjoyed an excellent steak and lobster meal.

She met the Devil, who was actually a really nice guy (kinda cute). The conversation was spirited, and she never laughed so hard in her life. In fact, she was having such a good time that before she knew it, it was time to leave. Everybody shook her hand

and waved goodbye as she got on the elevator. The elevator went up, up, up. St. Peter awaited her.

"Now it's time to spend a day in Heaven," he said. And for twenty-four hours, she lounged on clouds, caught a harp concert, and listened to a choir of angels. She had a great time, and before she knew it, her twenty-four hours were up.

"So, you've spent a day in Hell, and you've spent a day in Heaven," said St. Peter when they met again. "Now you must choose your eternity."

The woman paused, and then replied, "Well, I never thought I'd say this. I mean, Heaven has been really great and all, but I think I had a better time in Hell."

So St. Peter escorted her to the elevator, said so long, and she went back to Hell. This time, when the doors of the elevator opened, the executive found herself standing in a desolate wasteland covered in garbage and filth. Her friends were there, but dressed in rags, and they were picking up garbage and putting it in sacks. The Devil came up to her and put his arm around her.

"I don't understand," stammered the woman. "Yesterday I was here and there was a golf course and a country club, and we ate steak, and we danced and had a great time. Now there is a wasteland of garbage, and all my friends look miserable."

The Devil smiled. "Yesterday, we were recruiting you," he said. "Today you're staff."

What the executive did—playing golf at the country club, talking with old friends, and eating a steak dinner—was an illusion. That's the way I see much of the hiring process. What you see is rarely what you'll get.

A law firm takes their summer interns on river rafting trips, but it's an illusion. Young attorneys must bill clients for forty to fifty hours a week and are promoted accordingly.

A car dealership promises its top salespeople the use of a new car. But a salesman must still sell ten to twenty cars a month to keep his job.

Whether it's golfing parties or steak dinners, stock options or signing bonuses—all that glitters may not be gold.

Why do I say this?

Because I'm a psychiatrist who has spent thirty years discerning the difference between appearances and reality. I look at people's exteriors, but I also hear what they have in their hearts.

Fifteen years ago I shifted my focus and began consulting to organizations about executive evaluation and managing change. If this shift seems like a stretch—switching from individuals to institutions and from couples to corporations—I didn't see it that way. It seemed like an opportunity to continue playing to my strengths.

As a financial whiz can look at a company's financial data, scan reams of computer printouts, and find the buried treasure (or trash) within a few minutes, a good psychiatrist can look into a person and see what that person holds inside.

What has this got to do with business?

Everything.

Because the secret in business today is not money or technology or ideas. It's people—really good people. And when it comes to hiring good people, the process is like a marriage. There's the courtship (the recruitment), the proposal (the offer), and the marriage (the job itself), which tends to change after the honeymoon is over, just like the landscape did in "A Cautionary Tale."

It's never a question of *if* problems will arise, but *what* those problems will be. If you haven't discovered any problems during your job search, you're missing something.

And therein lies the game. Both you and the interviewer are playing to win. You may be a chess player predicting your opponent's next move; or a soccer player shooting at the goal; or Sherlock Holmes following the clues to solve a mystery. Whatever the game, your challenge is twofold in the hiring process:

☞ **To find out what you need to know about the company.**

☞ **To convey that you are the "best and brightest" among the competition.**

In the following pages, I offer an insider's view of how to "read" the hiring process—just as any good therapist reads a client. Once you know what's really going on, you'll have more choices in the games companies play.

In one of the most memorable scenes in the film *Dead Poets Society*, a young teacher jumps up on his desk and explains, "I stand on my desk to constantly remind myself that we must look at things in a different way. You see, the world looks very different from up here. And if you don't believe me," he says, "come and see for yourselves."

As the students gaze out at their old, familiar classroom from up on his desk, this extraordinary teacher says, "Just when you think you know something, you have to look at it a different way. Even though it may seem silly or wrong, you must try. Dare to strike out. Dare to find new ground."

That is the purpose of this book. If you are willing to get up on the desk and see the world differently, the following tips should prove helpful.

As in my previous book, *Hiring Smart* (Ten Speed Press, 1998), I have three goals in the pages that follow.

First, I want to demonstrate several practical methods for getting the job you want. These methods will help to level the playing field and to lessen the anxiety of most job searches. Some basic strategies ("Write the Perfect Resume") may be old hat for the seasoned veteran, and you're welcome to skip forward at your own pace. Some methods ("Do Lunch or Be Lunch") apply more to executives than to hourly workers, but you can adapt these strategies to suit yourself.

Second, I hope that you'll come away with at least three new ideas. Try these ideas the next time you're in the job market. If they feel right, that's great. If not, pick another three and try again.

Third, I also expect that you'll save significant time, money, and energy in your next search. By weeding out jobs you don't want ("Do Your Homework"), you're more likely to put yourself on the A-list of those jobs you do want.

I've organized my ideas into sections on pre-interview strategies, interview strategies, and post-interview strategies. I've also included a summary chart that I hope you'll find helpful for quick reference.

Each section begins with a piece of conventional wisdom that was popular in its day. Conventional wisdom looks like common sense and is accepted as the way things are. The conventional path is often a good one—but there are less-common routes to follow too. The purpose of this book is to remind you that the "conventional" way isn't always the only way, and to encourage you to try some of the more unconventional ideas that follow.

And remember—these are games. So have fun with this book, and good luck!

Pre-Interview Strategies

"Everything that can be invented has been invented."

Michael Jordan won six World Championships and five Most Valuable Player awards with the Chicago Bulls. Jordan led the league in scoring ten times, the most ever. His 31.5 points per game is the highest regular season average in the history of the National Basketball Association. As Magic Johnson once said, "There's Michael—then there's the rest of us."

Jordan's athletic talents—the soaring leaps, daring fakes, sensational shooting, and smothering defense—are well known to most sports fans. But less well known is Jordan's preparation. Before the game Jordan would come into an empty, cold United Center in Chicago and practice for four hours, alone.

Like Michael Jordan, your preparation should begin long before the hiring game officially starts.

I've organized the pre-interview strategies into the preparation phase, practical steps, and more tips before the interview starts. This first part is about how best to work your way into the good companies, while leaving the bad— and ugly—ones for other job hunters. Put another way: These initial ten strategies will give you a few more ways to recognize whether you're being recruited for Heaven or Hell.

No. 1 Do Your Homework

The Game:

In real estate it's said that the three most important factors are location, location, and location. In job interviews, it's preparation, preparation, and preparation.

The Strategy:

A fundamental part of your preparation, preparation, preparation should be research, research, research.

Jim Ansara, CEO of Shawmut Design and Construction in Boston, says, "You cannot do enough preparation before the interview. I'm most impressed when some one has really dug into who we are and what we do. I'm turned off by someone who claims to have looked into our company but has done very little preparation, and gets it wrong. There's no better clue that someone has no idea why they're here than when they tell us they're really interested in design. Our name is Shawmut Design and Construction. But we haven't done any design for over five years."

Your preparation is like any good market research—know your customer. Is this attention to detail necessary? Definitely.

What you've found out about a company on the Web or in their stores is infinitely more interesting to discuss in an interview than such questions as "Where do you want to be in five years?" or "Tell me about your strengths and weaknesses." And if you've gone to the trouble of doing some research, you're more likely to have the former discussion than the latter.

Take the example of a Midwestern board of trustees that is interviewing candidates for college president, a job that pays $220,000 per year. One of the finalists (on his own time, with his own money) visits the college and takes notes on the physical plant—especially the library, science building, and a new performing arts center. His summary distinguishes him from the other five finalists who have read only the college's brochures, scanned its Web site, and commented on these sanitized versions of the college's history and story. His references check out, his thirty-year track record fits the college's needs, and he gets the job.

On these two pages you'll see how one candidate, in advance of his interview with a venture capital (VC) firm,

Pros

- I was able to access the Web site on the first try. Often, the servers for many VC Web sites are down, making the sites difficult to access.

- The Web site is very user-friendly. It is easy to navigate through the site. Headings on the home page clearly direct the user to the section they are looking for.

- The site is good at "retaining" visitors by making it very easy to get back to the Web site, even when one clicks through to a portfolio company's Web page. I can always get back easily to the VC Web site.

- The search engine and the site map facilitate the quick finding of material on the Web site. Not all VC Web sites have search capabilities.

- Your domain name matches the firm name, thereby making it intuitive for a user to locate and remember the URL.

e-mailed his detailed summary of its Web site "pros" and "cons"—which had taken about three hours to prepare—with his cover letter and resume.

Do you think he stood out from the competition? You bet.

Cons

- While the firm's URL is intuitive, research has shown that visitors are less likely to visit Web sites that have domain names greater than 8 characters (excluding the general part of the domain name). Your name is 12 characters long.

- This site does not have real audio or video clips embedded in the site, features that some of the top Web sites have.

- In general, the site is static. Making the site more dynamic, or "appear" to be more dynamic, would liven up the site and make the experience more interactive—and memorable—for the user.

- The site lacks reference quotes from portfolio company CEOs regarding your firm.

- The graphic used on the home page could be visually more appealing. (This is personal opinion, of course.)

- The "portfolio highlights" part of the Web site is currently incomplete.

Before a possible interview with Levi-Strauss for a sales position, another candidate did the following preparation on her own time:

- **She researched the major news Web sites such as "Business Week" and "Fortune" for current stories on the company.**

- **She went to Levi's local stores, including their online store, and became a consumer of their products. She spent about $100 on jeans, and she talked with salespeople about who their customers were, and what they were buying. Were Levi's products hard or easy to sell? Were they fun or boring? She also talked with managers of several stores about their relationship with Levi's over the years and what they thought the company was doing right and wrong.**

- **She looked at Levi's advertising.**

- **She went to Levi's Web site and got a good feel for their visual image.**

- **She identified key competitors.**

- **She talked to people in Levi's stated demographic group— the under-twenty-five-year-olds at coffee shops and schools. She asked them what jeans they wear, what they thought of Levi's jeans, and why. And she collected some terrific anecdotes from all these experiences.**

The candidate mentioned several of these experiences in her cover letter. Afterwards, she used the information in an interview, and then she was hired.

There are many ways to do your homework. The first

candidate went to the VC's Web site. The second candidate went to the Levi's Web site, as well as their stores and demographic group. Did these two candidates stand out from the competition? Absolutely.

You can also check out a Web site that offers insider information on companies. There are many such services out there, but two particularly good ones that I am familiar with are Wetfeet.com, "The Information Source for Job Seekers," and VaultReports.com, whose slogan is "Bitch about your boss."

Let's say that you use Wetfeet.com. Through it you can read about a company's competitive strategy, industry position, history, organization, products, services, technology, technical program management, operations, customer service, production, editorial policies and procedures, business development, marketing, and finances, usually in less than fifty—often well-written—pages!

As VaultReports put it in a letter to me: "I think you'll appreciate the savvy, lively style of our writers, who spend day and night interviewing 'infiltrators' that we've established at leading companies across the country."

The cost of this research gold mine is $25. Is researching the job you want worth $25?

If you're seriously considering working for a particular company, also do a Lexis-Nexis/Dun and Bradstreet search before your interview starts to determine if the company has any outstanding legal problems. Here's why.

I have a friend who was hired by a fellow she knew personally, and he turned out to be a less than honorable character. After the debacle, she learned that his professional history included broken promises, constant investigations, and repeated lawsuits—which were all part of the public record and available through the Internet. Much of her predicament could have easily been avoided.

So "Doing Your Homework" means not only being informed about a company, but seeing if the organization has any skeletons in the closet that you should be aware of.

Personality Type No. 1 The Perfectionist

The Perfectionist tends to be reasonable, responsible, and respectable. These types are also decisive in practical matters, driven by both a sense of responsibility and bottom-line behavior. If one word could describe The Perfectionist it would be "dependable."

Possible Strengths

Ability to:

- Allow people their privacy for uninterrupted work
- Get things done steadily and on schedule
- Be strong with detail and careful in managing it
- Have things at the right place at the right time
- Honor commitments and follow through
- Work well within an organizational structure

Potential Weaknesses

May:

- Overlook the long-range implications in favor of day-to-day operations
- Neglect the interpersonal side of life
- See the future in overly negative terms; be unduly pessimistic
- Become rigid in their ways and be thought of as inflexible
- Get stuck and not see alternative ways to solve problems

The Prayer

Lord, help me to begin relaxing about little details tomorrow at 11:41:32 A.M.

Network, Network, Network

Most of the best jobs are not advertised—any-where.

Take a hint from the company. "Casting a Wide Net" is how they attract the big and little fish. You too can (and should) play the Network Game.

Calvin Coolidge, of all people, observed, "Nothing in the world can take the place of persistence. Talent will not; nothing is more common than unsuccessful men with talent. Genius will not; unrewarded genius is almost a proverb. Education will not; the world is full of educated derelicts. Persistence and determination are omnipotent."

Persistence means telling everyone you know that you're in the job market. "Everyone" includes friends, family members, colleagues, classmates, career centers, sorority sisters, fraternity brothers, teachers, ex-teachers, neighbors, doctors, dentists, clergymen, clergywomen, bankers, lawyers, accountants, bookkeepers, phone contacts, e-mail contacts, industry contacts, civic groups, support groups, volunteer organizations, and anyone else who might help in your job search.

After leaving her company, a fundraiser stayed in contact with her assistant. Ten years and a number of job changes later, the former fundraiser launched a freelance-writing business. She struggled through a difficult first year, but then her former assistant—now a good friend who just happened to be a high-level executive at a leading discount brokerage firm—set her up with a number of very lucrative long-term projects. Although the word "networking" never came up, it was a classic example of one friend helping another friend.

A few years ago, I worked with Quad Graphics, a world-class printing company. Today, they employ 12,000 people.

Of that total, 6,360 are related by blood or marriage—a full 53 percent of Quad's workforce got their jobs because of a family network.

TravelSmith is a travel clothing and accessories catalog business founded in 1993 that plans to go from $75 million in sales and 150 employees last year to $200 million in sales and 300 employees next year. At a seminar for their managers, we were discussing "best practices" before the interview. We asked the participants: "How did you come to work here?" Everyone was astonished that the great majority had come to TravelSmith from personal references, hearing about the company from a friend or colleague.

Following our review of standouts and washouts, the managers realized what worked and didn't work at TravelSmith. More specifically, the company—about to double in size and revenue—learned that the key to great hires was networking within the company. (This is true of most successful organizations I know.)

About 85 percent of job seekers and career changers find employment through colleagues, classmates, associates, acquaintances, friends, and family members. So make a list of everyone you've ever known. Edit it later. Once you know exactly what kind of job you're interested in, look through the list for names of people to enlist in your cause and let them know you're looking. Give them a call or write an e-mail. Then you should also send them a resume, a bio, or business card.

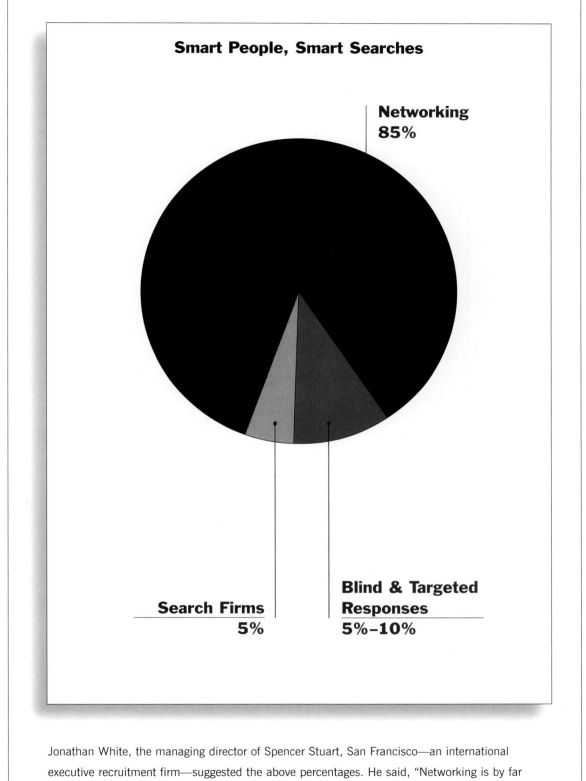

Smart People, Smart Searches

**Networking
85%**

**Search Firms
5%**

**Blind & Targeted
Responses
5%–10%**

Jonathan White, the managing director of Spencer Stuart, San Francisco—an international executive recruitment firm—suggested the above percentages. He said, "Networking is by far the most effective strategy for finding a job."

Master E-Mail

As the telephone is a necessity for Hollywood agents, the Internet and e-mail are necessary for most job applicants. Employers may use these electronic tools to discover how adept you are with them.

Get connected. Become competent at using e-mail and the Internet.

With International Data Corporation estimating that in the year 2000, 90 million workers in the United States will send 2.8 billion e-mail messages a day, the Internet is a major issue for the job hunter.

After posting a job opportunity at the start-up Internet company where he works, my son received twenty-five resumes. He scanned the resumes and twelve stood out. Because e-mail was a critical part of the job, he wondered how comfortable these candidates were in that medium. How quickly would they respond to e-mail? Then he e-mailed the twelve candidates three questions to which he would await an answer before he scheduled an interview. "Please give me your thoughts via e-mail within one week," he wrote the twelve candidates. His three questions were:

☞ **What's your experience with the Internet?**

☞ **What do you think of our Web site?**

☞ **What's your favorite movie?**

Within a week, my son had received two responses. Ten didn't answer at all. One reply read, "Thanks for the time you took in reviewing my resume. I look forward to speaking to you soon. Here are my thoughts in answer to your three questions…"—and his replies were terrific. Who do you think my son called for an interview?

I suggest that you conduct at least some of your initial correspondence by e-mail. A good strategy is to send your resume, follow up with a phone call, then send an e-mail if you don't get a response. If you rely only on voice mail to reach busy people, you'll never hear from many potential employers because of their incredibly hectic schedules. Whereas many employers, especially in start-ups and fast-paced companies, do check their e-mail and are very good at responding to it.

E-mail is only one part of the Internet tidal wave. Today, time-honored traditions are changing fast. In 1999, for example, sixteen ambitious engineers offered to sell their services on the auction site eBay for a starting bid of over $3.14 million. Ultimately they withdrew their offer, but the notion of people auctions on the Web was born. As one computer programmer concluded, "With a talent auction it's a lot easier than sending in a resume. It's not just for techies."

Gone are the days when offers were sealed with handshakes. Technology and a tight labor market are combining to usher in an era of e-cruiting, virtual interviews, and even talent auctions. Offers are almost instantaneous. The rules are changing. You can't afford to be left out.

The previous three strategies will ensure that you don't waste too much time going to an interview you don't really want. In the next two strategies, you'll learn more about wooing your A-list for the jobs you *do* want.

But first, look at the diagram on the following page, which outlines steps you should take to ensure a phone call—or e-mail—back.

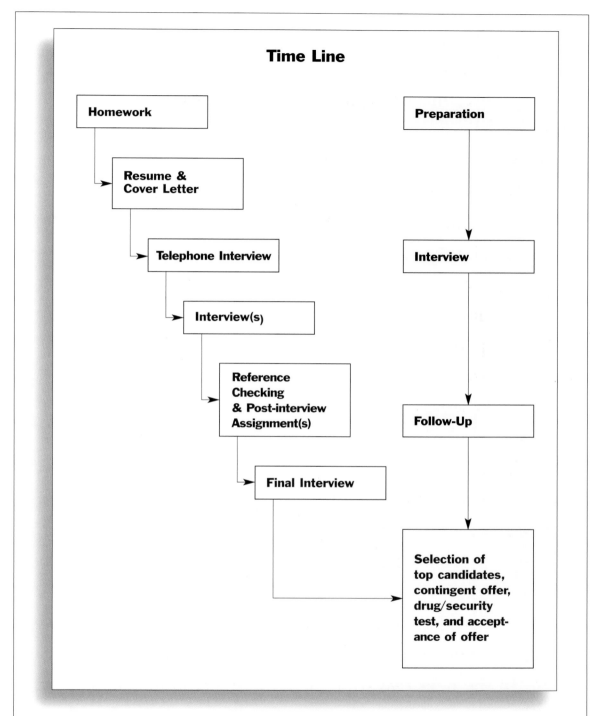

Time Line

Homework → Resume & Cover Letter → Telephone Interview → Interview(s) → Reference Checking & Post-interview Assignment(s) → Final Interview

Preparation → Interview → Follow-Up → Selection of top candidates, contingent offer, drug/security test, and acceptance of offer

To successfully navigate all the stages of the job hunt, you must know the objective for each step, above, and you must complete each step to get to the next level. For example, your objective with the resume and personal cover letter is to get a phone call or e-mail back. You should write a resume that is not *War and Peace*—just the highlights—preferably one page. You must then complete step #2 to get to #3, step #3 to get to #4, and so forth.

Write the Perfect Resume

Assume that the reader puts your resume into one of three piles. In Pile A are candidates who will definitely get a return phone call. In Pile B are the maybes. In Pile C, the "no's."

You have no way of knowing if the reader will care about what school you graduated from, or what she'll think about the jobs you've had, or how long you stayed at those jobs —in other words, you can't ensure that you'll get into Pile A. But a few steps can keep you out of Pile C.

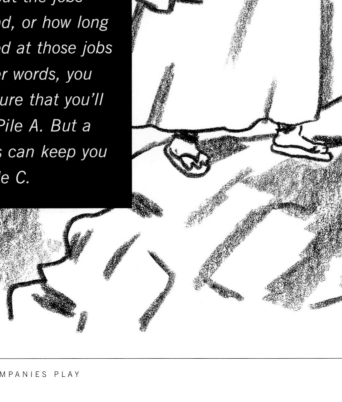

To paraphrase Winston Churchill: Never, never, never, never send out a resume that hasn't been reread a dozen times. And not just by you. Even the most experienced editors hand off their work to a second pair of eyes. They know that after reading the same material over and over, they'll miss a few errors.

If you don't catch misspellings and typos, you'll end up with such bloopers as "Worked party-time as an office assistant." Or "I am entirely through in my work; no detail gets by me." Or "Typing speed of 40–50 rpm." Or "Assisted with murders and acquisitions." (No joke. These are all documented errors found on job resumes.)

You have one chance to stand out. Make the most of it. Therefore, on the next page, you'll find my top ten list for writing a resume. ☛

Resumes
Top Ten List

1. KIS—Keep It Simple.

2. Start with name, address, phone and fax
   number, and e-mail address at the top.
   (Don't put the current date on the resume.)

3. Limit yourself to one page.
   Remember that the average reader will scan your
   resume in about ten seconds.

4. Use common headings, such as "education,"
   "objective," "skills summary," and "work experience."

5. Use any standard format and start
   with recent history. Use specific dates.

6. Use bullets or short paragraphs—four lines or less.

7. Quantify your success.
   ("Net revenues increased 100% in two years.")

8. Highlight your computer or Internet skills,
   even if you're not looking for a high-tech job.

9. Use a laser printer and good paper stock.

10. Have five people read and critique your draft.
    Then draft your final resume again.

In addition, you can show your ingenuity in other ways, especially if you're looking for a creative job.

Jeff Reifman believes that one reason Microsoft hired him when he was twenty was the *Calvin and Hobbes* cartoon he included on his resume. Nine years later, he's still operating in a quirky, offbeat way, splitting his time between his job and a nonprofit he founded to funnel profits back into the Seattle community where he lives.

My friend Chris Cornyn, who now runs his own ad agency, dreamed of being the creative director for Apple Computer. Where do you go from there? Chris sent his resume and creative portfolio to the Apple hiring office. Three weeks passed, and he heard nothing. So he went to the Apple parking lot in Cupertino, California, and plastered the windshield of every car in the lot with a one-page, self-promotional flyer. For three days he continued this insanity, and, yes, he got an interview.

On the next page, you'll see a variation on a recent Kinko's ad that is a good example of one picture being worth a thousand words—unconventional wisdom that works! ☛

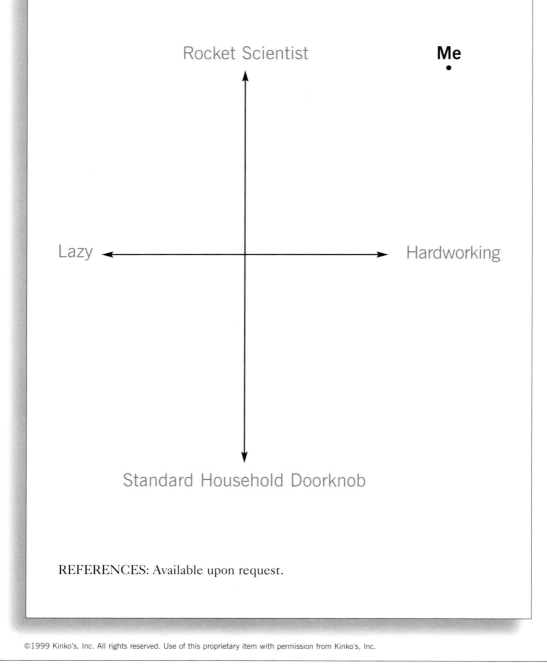

ROBERT ERVIN

936½ Hartswick Ave.   (805) 652-4022
State College, PA 16803

OBJECTIVE: To gain an entry-level position with a highly successful company.

Rocket Scientist

Me
•

Lazy ←——————————————→ Hardworking

Standard Household Doorknob

REFERENCES: Available upon request.

Personality Type No. 2

Here the primary desire is to be of service and to minister to individual needs. This type believes work is good, play must be earned. The Duty, Honor, Country Type is willing to work long hours. Any task, once undertaken, will be completed if at all possible.

Possible Strengths

Ability to:

- Provide security in a clearly structured, calm, quiet, efficient environment
- Apply experience to problems
- Take the practical needs of people into account
- Use strong follow-through skills in carrying out organizational goals
- Be painstaking and responsible with detail and routine
- Have things at the right place at the right time

Potential Weaknesses

May:

- Be overly pessimistic about the future
- Not be seen as sufficiently tough-minded when presenting views to others
- Be undervalued because of quiet, self-effacing style
- Not be as flexible as the situation and others require
- Get stuck and not see possible ways out

The Prayer

Lord, help me to be more laid back, and help me do it exactly right!

Personalize Your Cover Letter

The Game:

The company asks you for a one-page cover letter that describes your interest in the job.

The Strategy:

In this game, you want to provide a quick read with a personal hook that will set you apart from other applicants.

**S**eventy percent of candidates begin their cover letters, "I have decided that the time has come for me to review my options and seek more challenging opportunities. Upon careful review of my professional and personal goals, I am writing this letter...." Don't write such a letter. Do follow these basic guidelines:

☛ **Be clear and concise, and use a conversational tone.** During World War II, President Franklin D. Roosevelt received a memo that read, "Such preparation shall be made as will completely obscure all Federal buildings and non-Federal buildings occupied by the Federal government during an air raid for any period of time from visibility by reason of internal or external illumination."

"Tell them," FDR translated, "that in buildings where they have to keep the work going, to put something across the windows."

☛ **Don't depend on a spell check.** The computer can't distinguish "to" from "too" or "two," or "there" from "their" or "they're," and if you leave the "t" off of "the," a spell check won't pick up "he."

☛ **Limit yourself to half a page.**

☛ **Add "If I don't hear from you by** [a specific date], **I will call you the week of** [specific date]." **Then call.**

☛ **Sign the letter.**

That's sound advice, and it works. And now for the unconventional wisdom.

David O. Mann, a Naval Academy graduate, researched financial service companies before possible interviews. With his cover letter, he sent a one-page sheet summarizing his fitness reports from his last two jobs. This was to save the recipient from having to read more than necessary. Dave would also try to find out if the company employed any of the following people:

☞ **Someone who was both a Naval Academy and HGS (His Graduate School) alumnus/alumna.**

☞ **If not, a Naval Academy graduate.**

☞ **If not, anyone with a military background.**

☞ **If not, just an HGS graduate.**

Dave sent the cover letter and summary to one of the people above, not a generic address like the Human Resources Department. "These reports were effective because the person I sent them to was more likely to take the time to read them," he says, "and I always followed up with a phone call."

On the next page you'll find a one-page summary of the performance evaluations that David Mann included with his cover letter. See what you think.

Employment Evaluation Summary
Selected quotations from performance evaluations:

"Without a doubt, one of the top junior Supply Corps officers in the Navy today and my best all-around White House Liaison officer."

"He instinctively understands every phase of project management—planning, execution, follow-up and requires zero prompting to stay on track."
February 1, 1997—July 16, 1997,
The Honorable J.H. Dalton, Secretary of the Navy.

"My best action officer for all short-lead, high-pressure projects."

"Recognized expert on business and contracting issues... responded to all Presidential correspondence."
March 18, 1995—January 31, 1996,
The Honorable J.H. Dalton, Secretary of the Navy.

"#1 of 21 Division Officers of all ranks and designations on the USS *Mississippi.*"
February 1, 1995—March 17, 1995,
Captain W.J. Laz, Commanding Officer.

"Lieutenant Mann is the most talented young Supply Corps officer I have seen in my 25-plus years."
September 1, 1994—January 31, 1995,
Captain W.J. Laz, Commanding Officer.

How to personalize your cover letter?

Ask yourself: What do I have in common with a potential employer? It may be a mutual acquaintance ("Darcy Dakin suggested that I write you"), a school association ("I noticed that we both went to Swarthmore"), or a common background ("Like you, I also started working as a copy kid at a local newspaper").

If you don't have a personal contact, talk to an assistant before you write the letter. Then you can say, "I was talking with Maya, and she said that you were very busy, so I'm sending this brief summary and cover letter."

This personal sentence will almost always assure that your letter is read.

Personality Type No. 3

The Saint focuses on possibilities, thinks in terms of values, and comes easily to decisions. The small number of this type (1 percent) is unfortunate, since the Saint has an unusually strong drive to contribute to the welfare of others and genuinely enjoys helping other people.

Possible Strengths

Ability to:

- Empathize with other people
- Forecast how other people will (and do) feel
- Appreciate other people's contributions
- Follow through on commitments
- Work with integrity and consistency
- Provide opportunities for creativity
- Provide a harmonious, quiet environment with a personal feel

Potential Weaknesses

May:

- Find their ideas overlooked and underestimated
- Not be forthright with their criticism of others
- Be reluctant to intrude upon others and thus keep too much within themselves
- Operate with a single-minded concentration, thereby ignoring other tasks that need to be done

The Prayer

Lord, help me not be a perfectionist. (Did I spell that correctly?)

No.6 Prepare for an Initial Phone Call

The Game:

Before you meet, the interviewer calls you to request extra copies of your resume or confirm the time of your appointment. What was that all about?

The Strategy:

Don't get screened out before the interview. During the period that you're a job seeker, present a professional image at all times. No cute stuff.

**S**hould this matter? It usually does.

In any phone contact with your prospective employer, be enthusiastic and accommodating, and devote your full attention to the call. The employer may be checking out your phone skills. How articulate and enthusiastic are you? The caller may engage you in some conversation about the job in order to listen to how you respond, whether you hesitate when asked if you'll be free to work late on some nights, and so forth.

When my wife was looking for an office manager, one top candidate's first question on the phone was "I've just come back from England. What kind of health insurance do you have?" And then he put my wife on hold. As you can imagine, my wife saved herself an office interview.

Of course, there are con men who have a terrific phone presence and some good candidates who are awkward on the phone. So if you are uncomfortable on the phone—assuming you're not applying for a job as a telephone receptionist, phone operator, or a telemarketer—let your listener know that. If a phone call at work will compromise you, be sure to make that clear. "I can't talk at work, but here's my home number. Feel free to call me any evening or weekend." This is an honest and above-board statement that is almost always appreciated.

Expect Changes in Interview Schedules

Companies may change interview arrangements because of "scheduling problems." Such changes may also have a hidden agenda.

Pay attention when an interviewer changes the interview arrangements. Be flexible. A change in plans can tell the interviewer more than most questions he can ask in an interview.

Danny Stern is president of Leigh Bureau, a premier speakers' agency that represents such business superstars as Peter Drucker, Michael Porter, Lester Thurow, Harriet Rubin, and Nicholas Negroponte. This story is one that Danny told me about Bob Greenberg, a professor at the San Francisco Conservatory of Music, who speaks on music appreciation.

Danny had flown in from New Jersey to hear Bob, and Bob naturally hoped for a flawless audition, but it was not to be. Thirty minutes before his lecture, Bob Greenberg's audiovisual equipment was nowhere in sight—no microphone, no loudspeakers, no sound equipment for the audience awaiting his lecture. Danny was as interested in how Professor Greenberg handled the crisis as in how he delivered the lecture. He remained calm, kept his sense of humor, and worked with the hotel staff to solve the problem. Ultimately, his equipment found its way to him with just minutes to spare.

Had Bob Greenberg been mediocre, or even a good speaker, Danny Stern might not have been interested in representing him. However, Greenberg not only spoke well, but now Danny knew that he was capable of grace under pressure. His flexibility said more about his ability to handle adversity than Danny could ever have learned with clever questions in an interview. Danny Stern wanted not only great speakers, but good people too. And with twenty years in the business, he had had his share of big egos, and he no longer wanted to represent prima donnas. Bob Greenberg was clearly not that.

Why is flexibility so important?

Because things happen, especially if you're auditioning for a new role.

One of my daughters, Sara, is an actress in Hollywood, and I recall a time she was stuck in traffic on the San Diego Freeway during rush hour on her way to the Los Angeles International Airport. As she ran toward the boarding gate, she was paged by her slightly hysterical agent. Could Sara change her plans and re-audition that night for a role on *Friends*?

Sara turned around and took a cab to NBC's Burbank studios. Although a big-name actress also auditioned and got the role, the casting agent appreciated Sara's flexibility and called her the following week for another plum part.

The take-away lesson is this: Anytime you have occasion to demonstrate your flexibility for a potential employer— do it. Consider the exercise an obvious audition for a permanent role.

P.S. A schedule change that allows you to meet a higher level executive than originally planned is a clear signal that you are doing very well. Conversely, a shorter schedule—"We regret that Mr. Jones is no longer available this afternoon"— or a schedule change to a lower level interview is usually a flashing yellow light.

Personality Type No. 4   The Independent Thinker

The Independent Thinker is the most self-confident of all the types. Decisions come naturally to this type; once a decision is made, they are at peace. After all, they know they're right!

Possible Strengths

Ability to:

- Encourage individuality and support autonomy
- Be creative and ingenious, seeing new possibilities for old problems
- Tackle new problems with great enthusiasm
- Push the organization to understand the system as a whole
- Allow and understand people's need for privacy
- Stay focused and get results
- Organize ideas into action plans
- Visualize what the organization can be
- Create an environment for decisive, intellectually challenging people focused on implementing long-range visions

Potential Weaknesses

May:

- Get stuck on details, especially if tired
- Overdo potentially addictive activities (food, alcohol, exercise, etc.)
- Appear so stubborn that others are afraid to approach or challenge them
- Criticize others and themselves severely in striving for an ideal
- Have difficulty letting go of impractical ideas
- Ignore the impact of their ideas or style on others

The Prayer

Lord, keep me open to others' ideas, WRONG though they may be!

Start with the Receptionist

The Game:

It's not uncommon for a candidate to be evaluated in an informal way before the interview officially begins.

The Strategy:

The evaluation starts as soon as you walk through the door. Pay close attention to receptionists, assistants, and secretaries.

My secretary worked twenty-three years for a federal judge. The judge, law clerks, and secretary formed a close-knit team, almost like a family. Teamwork was absolutely crucial. Those staff members who saw candidates before the interview helped to determine who would or wouldn't be hired.

The secretary's office was where candidates sat and waited to be interviewed by the judge. These candidates, who were second-year law students, tended to be the best and the brightest in America—the top 5 percent of the top five law schools. Book smart and test smart, these men and women wrote brilliantly and were often editors of their schools' law reviews. Nonetheless, there were better and worse candidates when it came to behavior.

The usual pleasantries would be exchanged, and my secretary, Suzanne, would ask a few questions, such as "How was your trip to San Francisco?" or "How do you like law school?"

All these candidates were undoubtedly nervous about their upcoming interview with a federal judge, but the better candidates were able to converse, laugh, and act like real people in Suzanne's office. When the judge came to take these individuals into his chambers, they often turned to Suzanne and waved or said, "Good talking with you."

But other candidates had trouble meeting Suzanne's eyes during their wait. They might manage a short, obligatory answer, or they might project a condescending attitude toward her, constantly looking around to see what the law clerks in the adjacent office were doing, to see what was really happening in the judge's chambers. At this point, Suzanne would often stop trying to engage such candidates, and they would sit in silence. She believed that she didn't exist in their minds, and I'm sure she didn't.

For these particular candidates, their final downfall was in leaving the judge's chambers after the interview, shaking hands and saying goodbye to everyone except Suzanne. "I doubt these clerk applicants ever realized what a faux pas they had just made in my office," Suzanne told me. "Why these highly intelligent people wouldn't think that an assistant would discuss their behavior with the judge, I'll never know. Of course, they never got the job."

What applies for secretaries and assistants is also true for receptionists.

Several years ago, I spoke to the Harvard Business School admissions office. Knowing that Harvard gets almost 9,000 MBA applications for about 900 openings, it has its pick of applicants. Great schools. Great resumes. Usually great jobs, too, following school. Often these candidates end up at a Wall Street firm or with a coveted overseas assignment for a multinational corporation.

Whether the candidates have to leave their job and fly from Tokyo or Nairobi, they rarely decline an invitation to come to Harvard, even for a half-hour interview. And who arranges the logistics? Receptionists. I suggested that we ask these key people what they thought of each applicant based on their telephone contacts.

Some candidates were terrific, we learned. It took one call to arrange everything. But other candidates, who might have been extremely articulate and charming in person with an admissions officer, were downright rude to the receptionists on the phone.

Since these MBA candidates were the world's future business leaders, my advice was to record their rudeness as part of the pre-interview process. It may not be common knowledge—or conventional wisdom—but you should know that the assistants' and receptionists' input is a crucial part of most good hiring decisions.

Observe the Clues in Front of You

Most interviewers will start selling as soon as the right candidate sits down. Observe the clues in front of you before the interviewer starts selling their organization.

Judge by what you see, not what they say. Remember, "The obscure we see eventually, but the obvious takes a lot longer."

The character Sherlock Holmes was based on a famous internist who taught Arthur Conan Doyle at Edinburgh Medical School—Dr. Joseph Bell. A master of observation and deduction, Dr. Bell would dip a finger into a foul-smelling liquid and then put his finger into his mouth in class, and he would instruct his students to do the same. As the students grimaced, Dr. Bell would point out that while he had placed his index finger into the awful brew, it was his middle finger that found its way to his mouth.

Take advantage of the time before the interview. For example, as you park your car, look at the organization's parking lot, if it has one. Are there reserved executive parking spaces? Is the lot filled with Fords or BMWs? Are they clean or dirty? With bumper stickers or without? And if the cars have bumper stickers, do they say "Question Authority" or "Support Your Troops Abroad"? These details can tell you a lot about the organization you're dealing with, or what kind of people visit the place.

So too with office space. A low-rent start-up sends one kind of message; a blue-chip business with Persian rugs on the floor and original paintings on the wall sends a different message. Some offices have a hierarchy and doors with nameplates for executive vice-president, senior vice-president, and vice-president.

Some offices have a buzz; other offices are so dead that a cannon could go off and no one would notice. Some receptionists act friendly, offer you coffee, and make you feel welcome. Others don't. Some telephone operators answer on the first ring; others don't.

Be clear about what you want. Then look for clues as to its existence. For example, if you want a fast pace and advancement, look at the ages of executives. If you want a hierarchy, look for those reserved parking places and name-plates. If you want a bottoms-up organization, see if the receptionist treats the president just like everyone else.

Such clues will tell you a lot about a company, and much more than you'll learn from a sales pitch by an interviewer.

When my youngest daughter, Mara, interviewed for a newspaper publisher, the company was moving into new offices and everything was in total chaos. The publisher himself, in suit and tie, was helping the workmen carry the old tables into the new space. In those few seconds, Mara saw what kind of boss she'd be working for, and she was right.

Right Clues, Wrong Man

It's important to keep in mind that some clues can lead us in the wrong direction. For example, it's time to elect a world leader, and your vote counts. Here's the scoop on three leading candidates.

Candidate A:

Associates with corrupt bosses and consults with astrologists.
Has had two mistresses.
Chain smokes and drinks eight to ten martinis a day.

Candidate B:

Was kicked out of office twice.
Sleeps until noon.
Used opium in college.
Drinks a quart of brandy every evening.

Candidate C:

Is a decorated war hero.
Eats a vegetarian diet.
Doesn't smoke.
Drinks an occasional beer.
Hasn't had any extramarital affairs.

Which of these candidates is your choice?

Candidate C is Adolph Hitler.
Candidate B is Winston Churchill.
Candidate A is Franklin D. Roosevelt.

Know That Most Companies Have Biases

The company knows all about the importance of a diverse workforce. However, they can't always control their interviewers, who may feel more comfortable hiring people like themselves.

Proceed with caution. If you have concerns but really want the job, it may not help your cause to ask, "Mr. Jones, what is being done to change the Texaco culture to be more sensitive to diversity?"

During the pre-interview preparation and interview itself, your job is to figure out the prejudices of a company, if you can.

How do you do that?

First, there's the public record, which can be gleaned from doing your homework. If you were checking out Texaco or Denny's, for instance, you'd find disturbing headline stories in recent media reports. Second, there's also a company's track record. Look around the office and ask yourself: Does this organization have a diverse workforce? (Very few do.) In multicultural America, this is an issue.

In California, where I live, Asians make up 6 percent of the population, but at the University of California at Berkeley, Asians represent 39 percent of the incoming class. Latinos make up 11.3 percent of the U.S. population, but in California, 40 percent of the population under 18 years old is Latino. By 2050, it's estimated one out of every four people in the United States will be Latino.

In America, business schools are aware of these demographic realities. Wharton had 17 percent minorities in their incoming class in 1997, Harvard had 18 percent, and Stanford had 25 percent. These numbers don't include the foreign students who account for an additional 25 percent of incoming classes. This means that 40 to 50 percent of today's top business school students are either foreign born or from minority American backgrounds.

Several years ago, a public service ad for the Urban Alliance on Race Relations won a Clio Award. (The Clios are the Academy Awards for the best TV and radio advertising, worldwide.) In this ad, a young African-American male with a shaved head and unsmiling face appears on the screen. To the beat of music and what sounds like someone being lashed, the following words are slowly scrolled down the screen:

Michael Conrad.

Male.

Age 28.

Armed Robbery.

Assault and Battery.

Rape.

Murder.

Apprehended

August 1994 by

Police Lieutenant

Joseph Cruthers.

SHOWN HERE.

Urban Alliance on Race Relations

This ad demonstrates how fast most of us project our prejudices about gender, youth, and skin color, and how quickly we assume that a young black male is the criminal rather than the policeman.

Here's a story that should be a lesson to us all.

Several years ago, during her junior year at Woodrow Wilson High School in San Francisco, a fifteen-year-old gang member named Solaria was recommended by one of her teachers to a program that sends adolescents with leadership potential on summer programs worldwide. That summer, on a full scholarship, Solaria went to Cornell University to study rhetoric and debate. When she returned to Woodrow Wilson High that fall, she was elected student body president.

Upon graduation, Solaria received a full scholarship to attend the prestigious Northfield Mt. Hermon School in Massachusetts for a post-graduate fifth year of high school. And today, having just graduated from Brown University with a degree in economics and political science, Solaria has started an analyst job with Chase Manhattan Bank in New York City.

A board member of the organization that recognized Solaria's potential was Dana Emory, who is a partner at Dodge and Cox, an investment partnership in San Francisco.

In 1998, Dana convinced her company to hire several inner-city students for summer internship positions. This step, an unusual one for Dodge and Cox, proved to be positive for everyone involved. The students brought a new energy to the company, and morale was raised among the employees. For the students, this first contact with the business world proved to be transformative. For example, Cang—an immigrant from Vietnam —thought he was locked out of the business world. His bias was that all good positions in business were filled by aging white males. During his summer internship at Dodge and Cox, Cang's limited view was challenged, and his prejudices proved obsolete.

Dana Emory's foresight in counteracting biases on both sides of the racial and economic divide proved to be a tremendous asset to her firm. Today, the mentoring program at Dodge and Cox is recruiting future employees from a variety of diverse backgrounds.

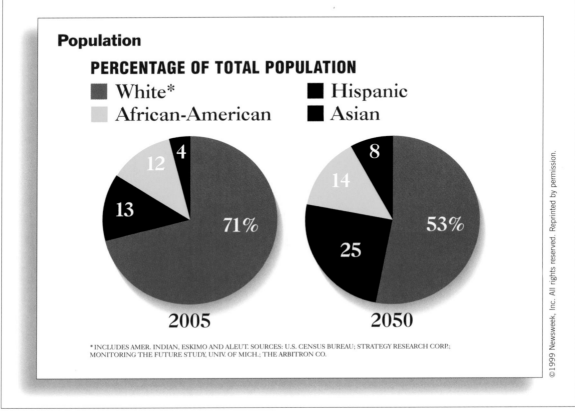

Population

PERCENTAGE OF TOTAL POPULATION

- White*
- African-American
- Hispanic
- Asian

2005: 71%, 13, 12, 4

2050: 53%, 25, 14, 8

*INCLUDES AMER. INDIAN, ESKIMO AND ALEUT. SOURCES: U.S. CENSUS BUREAU; STRATEGY RESEARCH CORP.; MONITORING THE FUTURE STUDY, UNIV. OF MICH.; THE ARBITRON CO.

There are four steps you should always consider when evaluating companies for biases.

1. **Do your homework.**

2. **Pay attention to what you see.**

3. **Look for companies that have summer internship programs.**
   If an organization has summer internships, it usually means that it is serious about recruiting a more diverse workforce.

4. **If possible, take an employee out for lunch or coffee and talk off the record.** What's his or her perspective on the company, in general, and on the company's biases, in particular? And how does the organization's unofficial attitude toward diversity affect its official policies and practices?

   Then you should use the information discreetly. Do not put Mr. Texaco on the spot about the alleged discrimination reported in the media. Use common sense.

   Good companies know that "perfect fit" no longer means "people like me." The best future employers will be comfortable with inclusivity, not exclusivity. The old elitism no longer equates with the Ivy League.

Strategies During
the Interview

"Who the hell wants to hear actors talk?"

—Harry Warner,
Warner Brothers, 1927

There's an old joke about an American opera singer who is invited to La Scala for her Italian debut. After her first aria, the audience shouts for an encore. So she sings the aria for a second time. Again, the crowd roars their approval, now with even more passion. So she sings it yet again. By the seventh time, the singer is exhausted and says very humbly, "Thank you so much. I am honored by your request, but I cannot sing it again." Whereupon a little voice from the back of the hall cuts through the stunned silence and announces, "You'll do it until you get it right."

That's pretty much how I feel about interviews. You keep auditioning until you get it right.

However, if you're on time with fingernails clean, hair combed, face scrubbed, shoes shined, appropriate attire, nice smile, and a bit of enthusiasm, it goes a long way. Most interviewers make a quick judgment based on your hand-shake, eye contact, facial expression, enthusiasm, and energy —in the first few seconds.

Then words take over—the interviewer's words forming the questions and your words forming the answers. During the interview, you're asked a series of predictable questions: What are your five-year goals? What are your strengths and weaknesses? Where have you made mistakes before? Where might you make mistakes again?

It reminds me of a *New Yorker* cartoon set in a public relations office where the PR director is explaining to a bewildered candidate, "We're interested in words, not deeds."

Well, deeds do count. A person's two- or twenty-year track record is infinitely more important that a two-minute impression or a two-hour interview. I don't mean to put down interviews, just put them in perspective. *Interviews test how well someone interviews.* They're good barometers of individual eloquence, ability to think on one's feet, and workplace chemistry. Although seeing a candidate in action would be the best of all possible worlds, *the interview is crucial. And it's what most companies go on to make a hiring decision.*

In this chapter, I'll describe some games companies play in that exhausting and unnatural ritual called the job interview, and suggest some strategies to deal with them.

Have Your Pitch Down Pat: The Three Basic Rules

"Be yourself. Maintain eye contact. Dress conservatively. Ask questions. Blah, blah, blah." To seal the deal you need to transform your interview from generic Q&A into a demonstration of your abilities.

In 1532 Machiavelli said that success depends on those matters over which you have control, not matters where you have no control.

I have three prescriptions that will give you more control in an interview. Although these ideas will not put you in the driver's seat, they will definitely help you navigate the hiring highway.

1. Talk isn't cheap, so don't wing it. You should answer commonly asked questions using the four S's. That is: *Make a statement, support the statement, summarize, and then shut up.* Your answer(s) should be about 20 seconds, and certainly no longer than two minutes.

For example, in answer to the off-beat question "When did you last get angry?" you could say, "With my boss during the budgeting process." You'd support that statement: "His numbers were unrealistic, and I told him so." And summarize, "So we strongly agreed to disagree." Then shut up.

2. It's not just what you say, but how you say it. Most interviewers listen to the music, as well as the words. In response to a question about your family, you could say, "That's an illegal question" (however, you probably won't get the job). But you could also say, "If you're asking if I'll be available to work nights and weekends, or if I'm willing to travel, the answer is 'Yes.'" In this case, it's both the substance of your answer and the style that impresses the interviewer.

3. Anxiety is part of the game. Expect it. Like breathing in and breathing out, anxiety is a natural reaction to a situation where you feel out of control. There are probably many reasons for your anxiety before an interview, beginning and ending with the pressure to get a job, especially if you're out of work. The interviewer controls not only the interview, but your destiny as well. Why wouldn't you feel nervous? Telling you to relax before an interview is like telling you to relax before a root canal.

If you're aware of what you do when you're anxious, it can help, so ask a spouse, partner, mentor, or close friend for honest feedback. Do you clam up when you're nervous? Do you become stiff and formal? Do you talk too much? If you're conscious of your behavior under stress, you may have some control over it.

Let's say that you talk too much when you're anxious. If the interviewer is silent for a few seconds, don't interpret the silence as criticism. Catch yourself. Don't race to fill the vacuum. Don't ramble on and on. Most interviewers will appreciate your brevity (and self-control) and will go on to the next question.

In addition, I'd suggest that you practice in advance; use a friend or professional to help you prepare for the interview; videotape your answers; and watch the videotape.

The take-away idea is this: Have your pitch down pat and adjust to the interview situation accordingly.

Personality Type No. 5 The Risk Taker

The Risk Takers are often fearless, risking themselves, despite threat of injury, more than any other types. Of all the types, they are the most likely to pit themselves, or their technique, against chance, odds, or fate. They thrive on excitement; they crave excitement each day.

Possible Strengths

Ability to:

- Act as troubleshooters
- Be good at analysis, especially in technical areas
- Find flaws in advance
- Hold consistently to policy, standing firm against opposition
- Function as a walking compendium of information
- Get things done in spite of the rules, not because of them
- Remain calm during crises and thus have settling effect on others

Potential Weaknesses

May:

- Not share important information; appear unconcerned to others
- Be hypersensitive; take criticism very personally
- Be too expedient and take shortcuts
- Appear indirect
- Have uncontrolled emotional outbursts; show anger or other emotions unexpectedly

The Prayer

Lord, help me to consider people's feelings, even if the odds are 100 to 1 against me!

Rule: **Read the Interviewer's Style**

The Game

Most interviewers find a technique that suits them and stick with it.

The Strategy

This game is like chess, and your goal is to base your moves on your opponent's style of play. If you read the interviewer's style accurately and adjust accordingly, you're guaranteed to be way ahead of the game.

There's no right or wrong way to interview candidates. Some interviews last an hour. Some last longer, some less. Some interviewers probe on-the-job qualifications. Others ask about personal values. Some people have faith in the candidate's self-portrait, while other people (myself included) assume there's usually something hidden behind the candidate's interview persona.

It's in your best interests to read the interviewer accurately. If the person is a killer, you have a choice about telling war stories of the time you went for the jugular. If he's a conservative fellow, regaling him with your student-radical days is an obvious lapse in judgment. If he's a nice guy, you can be a nice guy. If she's a Type A, you can be a Type A. (However, if you pretend to be a Type A personality and are hired because of it, you're going to prove a real disappointment if you turn out to be a Type B.)

Here's an example.

A company in Los Angeles once interviewed a financial candidate, and I was asked to fly in from San Francisco to attend the interview.

The candidate arrived on time, and after the usual pleasantries, the chief financial officer started the questioning. The CFO was very business oriented. "What are your strengths and weaknesses?" he asked.

The candidate said his greatest strength was leading

teams, and he told a story. While working at a major bank, he had gone over its books and found some serious discrepancies. "This group of executives wanted to wallpaper over the cracks," he said, "but I call 'em as I see 'em. Telling the truth," he said, "has been both a strength and a limitation for me."

Then it was my turn. My style is to ask more personal questions, but I began with, "Do you have any questions for us?"

This is usually the last question in most interviews, yet I thought it might tell us if the candidate had researched the company, and if he had any concerns about the job. The candidate adjusted quickly and asked good questions.

CFO: "Tell me about a leadership role you've had."

The candidate shifted again, and reviewed a past project, described his position as team leader, his contribution, and the results of his leadership.

Next it was my turn: "Aside from your resume, can you tell us a little about yourself?"

Over the next ten minutes, the candidate spoke passionately about his parents, brothers, sisters, schools, summers, marriage, children, and an illness from which his wife had just recovered. The man spoke about his values and how he practiced them.

CFO: "How do you go about getting information?"

Again, well prepared, the candidate outlined a five-step

process he follows when gathering data. He added a specific example and told us about alternatives he had considered, and the conclusion he had reached.

Then I asked: "When the company checks your background—what will be the surprises?"

The man spoke about a DUI he had received ten years previously and trouble with a boss five years ago.

That was it. We finished in about an hour. The candidate had shifted from one interviewer's style to another's with ease, grace, and clarity. And the CFO hired him.

Trust
Your Instincts

In five milliseconds to five minutes, on the basis of their initial impression, many interviewers will make a quick judgment, and so should you.

Chemistry—whether good or bad—is a two-way street. You too should determine what you think of the interviewer and the organization as a whole. Is this a place you want to spend ten hours a day for the next

Candidates have told me, "If I like the receptionist, I usually like the company," or "If the interviewer has read my resume, I usually like the interviewer," or "If I need the job, I usually like the interviewer."

But it's always more complicated than that.

The candidate considers himself the one who is trying to please the interviewer. But it helps to realize that the company is also a seller, aiming to please the right candidate with perks and parties. (Remember that dinner and dancing were Hell in the Cautionary Tale.)

We talk about the candidate's dress and enthusiasm, but what about the interviewer's dress and enthusiasm? What if the interviewer is tall or short, fit or fat, obnoxious or polite, articulate or inarticulate, prepared or unprepared, relaxed or tense? What if the interviewer is under 30, or over 60? Will it make a difference if he is on time or late?

If the interviewer is late, for example, and explains why—a last-minute phone call, a candidate who was tardy for a previous interview—it helps to hear that explanation because it has happened to all of us. But if the interviewer doesn't explain his tardiness, especially if he's very late, it says something about him, as well as the company.

In addition you should look for affirmative or declarative sentences in an interview. "Now, let me tell you about where the department or company is going..." or "We really have a great group to work with here..." or "I believe in rewarding people for performance…" All are indicators that the tables have turned to selling you.

Despite being nervous, you have a chance in a few minutes—especially at the beginning and end of an interview—to assess the situation. If there's still something nagging at you, it may just pay to investigate the source of your discomfort.

Perhaps your discomfort comes from something rather subtle, such as generational differences, that may be important in determining whether you should take the job.

For example, my parents came of age in the 1930s. They were marked by the Depression's themes of insecurity and uncertainty. They worked hard and played by the rules. For my older cousins who came of age in the 1940s, World War II shaped their lives. For me, it was the 1950s, the Eisenhower years of *Father Knows Best* and relative stability.

My wife's transformative years were in the 1960s. Student uprisings, political assassinations, and Vietnam were the influences in this decade, whereas our children grew up in the 1980s. When I ask, "What describes your decade?" They say, "Money, materialism, and—me!" Narcissism is the key word.

As you look around at the age group(s) employed by the company—Baby Boomers or GenXers, hippies or techies—ask yourself how that group's values might clash or blend with your own values. These factors are usually a good barometer of whether you'll be comfortable in taking or lasting in the job.

Personality Type No. 6 The Strong, Silent Type

For whatever reason, The Strong, Silent Type seems more inclined to the fine arts than the other types. But this type's temperament is very difficult to observe, even in artists, and so he or she is probably the most misunderstood of all the types.

Possible Strengths

Ability to:

- Act to ensure others' well-being
- Infuse a quiet joy into their work
- Bring people and tasks together by virtue of a cooperative nature
- Pay attention to the humanistic aspects of the organization
- Create an environment that is flexible, aesthetically appealing, and people-oriented

Potential Weaknesses

May:

- Be too trusting and gullible
- Not criticize others when needed
- Not see beyond the present reality
- Not be able to express feelings verbally
- Avoid confrontation and conflict
- Be too easily hurt and withdraw

The Prayer

Lord, help me to stand up for my RIGHTS! (If you don't mind my asking.)

No. 14 Recognize the Human Resources Game

The Game

If you're advised to interview with HR to get a job, be careful. Is the HR director a key player? Does she have the CEO's ear? Is the HR department a dead-end or a powerhouse within the company?

The Strategy

Most HR departments are looking for ways to disqualify you. In dealing with HR, the best defense is a good offense—so read the clues around you and recognize illusion and reality.

**A**s an applicant, you should be aware that most people in HR have a very different philosophy about filling positions than hiring managers do. Here's how it works.

A hiring manager goes to HR and says, "I need a Web designer." The HR person sets about finding two or three strong, viable candidates for the manager. Which two or three will be determined by their resumes and maybe reference checks. HR department recruiters are typically risk-averse and overburdened.

HR may run an ad in newspapers and magazines for a Web designer that generates 200 or more resumes. Minimally, this will require an hour or two to screen. To save time, and improve prospects for success, the HR manager will eliminate all but the very best resumes—call these Group A. Questionable resumes go into Group B and are considered only if the A's are exhausted. The remainder go to the wastebasket. The HR department's responsibility is to *screen out* rather than *screen in* candidates. It's synonymous with the profession.

Most HR departments aren't looking for "interesting" people, whom they may perceive to be "risks." They want to present qualified, sure bets. They're not likely to pass along candidates that are strong on potential but shy on experience.

In contrast, hiring managers usually have less experience in the art of competitive screening. They aren't likely to receive many resumes or candidate overtures. They also have a greater sense of urgency about filling the position.

A manager with a strong ego ("I know best") is an ideal target for a direct approach by the unproven or oddball candidate. The combination of the hiring manager's inexperience, urgency, and ego can work in a candidate's favor.

A candidate who is not a poster child for the position should send in two resumes—one to HR and one directly to the hiring manager, who is more likely to be positively affected by one's background, life experience, and education. The hiring manager is usually more willing to take a risk, knowing that he might find a stellar Web designer who is an unproven, but great raw talent.

If you are an untraditional candidate, these are the realities. A company may want your skills, but you may not appear on their radar screen without some fancy footwork. If you have a less traditional background, you may have a very difficult time getting past the initial screen of the HR department.

On the other hand, if you're thoughtful, direct, and ask good questions—"How do you plan to continue the 20 percent growth mentioned in your annual report? What will be the resistance?"—most interviewers are going to have trouble screening you out.

Caveat: A personal connection with the HR department may be to your advantage, depending on the quality of the connection. Even a referral from a non-hiring manager to HR is still better than no connection at all. HR does a lot of interviews as favors to managers and friends.

Personality Type No. 7 The Kinder, Gentler Type

This type presents a calm, pleasant face to the world and is seen as reticent and even shy. Although they demonstrate a cool reserve toward others, inside they are anything but distant. They have a capacity for caring that is not always found in other types. One word that captures this type is "idealistic."

Possible Strengths

Ability to:

- Be flexible, unbureaucratic, calm, and quiet
- Find a place for each person in the organization
- Be persuasive about personal ideals; draw people together around a common purpose
- Seek new ideas and possibilities for the organization
- Quietly push for organizational values
- Allow time and space for reflection

Potential Weaknesses

May:

- Delay completion of tasks because of perfectionism
- Be hypercritical in quiet ways
- Try to please too many people at the same time
- Not adjust vision to the facts and logic of a situation
- Spend more time in reflection than in action
- Take criticism very personally

The Prayer

Lord, help me to finish everything I sta

Understand the Real Question(s)

A good trial lawyer will tell a client before a court appearance, "Ask yourself, what's behind the other attorney's questions? Then gear your answers to avoid the traps."

Your job is to understand what, if anything, is behind commonly asked questions and to address the interviewer's REAL concerns in your answer.

**M**ost questions are really meant to evaluate how you'll perform on the job and fit in with the workplace. It's easy to ramble on about yourself and your goals, but understanding the interviewer's real question is the key to making a lasting impression.

For example, my editor at Ten Speed Press was applying for her first job at a book publishing company. She knew that it was common for frustrated writers to apply for editorial positions in the hopes of getting their work published. So when the editorial director asked the question, "What brings you to book publishing and editing?" she said, "You're probably wondering if I'm a frustrated writer—and yes, I do write creatively on my own time. But in fact I'm a natural editor. In high school I was the yearbook editor, and in college I copyedited a literary magazine and weekly newspaper, so I know I can do an excellent job for you."

Early in the interview, the young woman disarmed the interviewer's fears and did the work for the interviewer. Telling the interviewer exactly how her past experience fit with the present job, the young editor also got the position.

Here are four examples of common questions and their hidden agendas:

1. "Why are you leaving your current job?"
It's estimated that eight out of ten people leave old jobs because of bad bosses. Will you take the high road, or will you badmouth your current boss? Be diplomatic—stick to

the issues, not the personalities.

You should also stay away from trite phrases such as, "I want to grow as a person" or "I'm seeking a more challenging opportunity." Instead, you should start with an issue such as "It's a family business, and I'm not in the family." Or "My company has just been sold." Or "I helped the company from its start-up phase through a successful IPO, and I felt it was time to move on."

2. "What are your five-year goals?"

John Lennon once said, "Life is what happens to you while you're busy making other plans," and I agree. The interviewer probably wants to know if you'll be with his company in five years, so don't get into specifics. Don't bog down in details. If you're asked the time, you wouldn't tell someone how to build a watch. Have an under-twenty-second answer and start with the short term.

Good answer: "You can evaluate my work in three, six, or twelve months—and if it's excellent, we can decide how best to use my talents within the company." Bad answer: "In five years I want to be a vice-president making $300,000."

3. "What will it take to get you?"

In a negotiation, this is the opening gambit. You name your price. If it's too high, the negotiator will look shocked. If it's too low, he'll look shocked too. That's why it's called a game.

Try to stay away from compensation in the initial interview. Keep It Simple. But what to do if you're pressed about money?

One friend pushes all finalist candidates on compensation. Up front, he wants to know if the person is affordable. He suggests you say something like "Compensation is important to me. Look, I want to be paid commensurate with what I bring to the company, but more than that, the job needs to be the right fit for both of us. If we feel good about the fit, we'll work out the pay package." Regardless of compensation, and if it's true, you can also say: "I have other options, but I think your company is the best fit for me."

4. "If I make you an offer, will you accept?"

This game is played like the college admission's game. The organization doesn't want to make you an offer that you'll refuse, so the question is "Are you serious?" Therefore it's okay to ask, "Is this an offer?" If it is, you can accept it, reject it, or put it on hold. If you're unsure about your decision, it's also okay to say, "I'd like to think about it for a few days." Then talk with a confidant, close friend, spouse, partner, and if possible, a few people who have worked for the company.

For example, if you're interested in family-friendly issues, ask questions. What about day care, flextime, job sharing, and parental leave? With a little probing, you'll get beyond the company's public relations to its actual practices. Then you can decide if the job is right for you.

The next few examples will help you prepare for other specific questions you'll encounter in most interviews.

More Common Questions

What They Say	What They Really Mean
"How do you spend your day?"	"Tell me the specifics—answering phones, attending meetings, putting out fires, walking around the office—and I'll know a lot more about you."
"What is the biggest hurdle you've ever had to overcome?"	"Tell me a story that demonstrates your self-awareness, humility, and ability to overcome hardship."
"We'll be doing our due diligence—a thorough background check. What should we be prepared for?"	"Tell me any surprises I'll hear. Your facial expression or hesitation in answering might also tell me what I want to know."
"How are you going to lose money for me?"	"Tell me where you've made mistakes before. Where might you make mistakes again?"

Personality Type No. 8 The Problem Solver

The one word that captures the unique style of the Problem Solver is "architect"—the architect of ideas and systems. This type exhibits the greatest precision in thought and language of all the types; they tend to see distinctions and inconsistencies in thought and language immediately.

Possible Strengths

Ability to:

- Allow privacy;
  foster independence
- Design logical and
  complex systems
- Tackle complex problems
- Exhibit short- and long-range
  intellectual insight
- Apply logic, analysis, and critical
  thinking to issues
- Cut directly to the core issues
- Reward self-determination

Potential Weaknesses

May:

- Be too abstract and therefore
  unrealistic about necessary
  follow-through
- Overintellectualize and become
  too theoretical in explanations
- Focus overly on minor inconsistencies at the expense of
  teamwork and harmony
- Turn critical analytical thinking
  on people and act impersonally
- Express anger and other emotions
  unexpectedly and unpredictably
- Be hypersensitive to criticism
  and take it very seriously

The Prayer

Lord, help me be
less independent, but
let me do it my way.

No. 13 Discover the Real Problem(s)

The Game:

This is one of the more important games that companies play: The apparent problem is rarely the real problem that most organizations face. Like the Cautionary Tale, what you see and hear is often not what you get.

The Strategy:

Your job is to identify the underlying problem(s), and demonstrate that you're part of the solution.

I n the "Help Wanted" ad, why is the company advertising for a project manager? Maybe it's just acquired another company. Maybe the old manager had trouble with people, or got sick, or moved to Nebraska. There are probably twenty-seven other possibilities. Your job is to try to find the story behind the headline and propose a solution to the organization who has the problem.

There's almost *always* a story or a hidden agenda behind the headline.

Let's say that the company's old project manager couldn't oversee two corporate cultures merging into one. If you defined the problem correctly, you could then ask, "What's going to be the resistance—internally and externally—to blending two cultures into one organization?" Most interviewers would be impressed by the question, and you'd undoubtedly have a leg up on the competition.

> **HELP WANTED**
> Interior Designer/
> Project Manager.
> Min. 7 years experi-
> ence. Familiar with
> code ADA reqmts.
> Able to interface
> with architects,
> builders, designers.
> PC experience a
> plus. Must be a team
> player. Please fax
> resume to....

As a psychiatrist, I've known married politicians who frequent singles bars, successful actors who solicit street hookers, trial lawyers who are addicted to cocaine, and business people who seem to have it all, but are so depressed that they're contemplating suicide.

Let's take Sam Francke, who can't concentrate on his job—can't read reports, can't make decisions, can't stop feeling blue—so he calls for an appointment. With apologies to Woody Allen, my initial hour with Sam goes something like this:

"I'm having trouble concentrating."

"Why?"

"I'm tired all the time."

"Why?"

"I wake up every morning at 2 a.m.,
  but can't get back to sleep."

"Why?"

"I'm under a lot of stress."

"Why?"

"Money and other things like that."

"What other things?"

"Like my doctor's visit next week."

"What doctor's visit? Why are you seeing a doctor?"

"Because I'm anemic."

"Why are you anemic?"

"I'm not sure, but the doctor
  thinks I may have leukemia."

Bingo!

Sam Francke is worried that he might have a terminal illness. No wonder he can't sleep. Sam's insomnia is only the tip of the iceberg. By discovering the hidden agenda, I can now go on to discuss his fear of cancer, rather than talk about his money, marriage, or sleeplessness.

The same is true for all of us. Your job is to keep your eyes and ears open and—if possible—to pinpoint the underlying problem.

No.17 Predict the "Tell Me About Yourself" Question

The Game:

When the question is "What can you tell me about yourself?" it's important to know what the interviewer is interested in. The real question is "Tell me something I can't get from your resume or references."

The Strategy:

Tailor your answer to fit the interviewer and the position. Is the interviewer trying to get a sense of your organizational skills or flexibility? Are they looking for professional or personal history?

The conventional answer might just be a rehash of your resume: "I graduated from the University of California, at Berkeley, where I was a reporter for *The Daily Bear*. In addition, I had a part-time job in the marketing department at PowerBar, and I graduated with a 3.72 grade point average. So I learned to organize my time and prioritize my schedule and blah, blah, blah."

But if the real question is "Tell me something I can't get from your resume," there's an alternative at this point. You can always ask, "Is there anything you'd like more information about?"

For example, let's say you're interviewing for a pilot's job with the Blue Angels flying team, and the interviewer really wants to know, "Are you a risk taker?" If risk taking is the hidden question, you should probably mention your bungee jumping, motorcycle racing, and skydiving instead of talking about your GPA or saying, "I haven't had a speeding ticket in twenty years."

Also helpful in responding to the interviewer: Look around the office at your surroundings. For example, Robin Bradford, who runs her own staffing agency—the Bradford Staff—has original paintings on the wall and pictures of her two young children on her desk, coffee table, and bookshelf. Art and her children are Robin's passions. If you mention your own love of art or the volunteer work you do with kids, you can count on scoring points in such an interview.

On the other hand, let's say that you walk into an office and see a hunter's trophies on the wall—a boar's head, elk antlers, a deer head—and pictures of the interviewer with his cronies on a duck-hunting trip. Seldom are clues so obvious, but a look around this interviewer's office will offer hints about his passions. Use this information to your advantage—by mentioning that you used to love to go duck hunting with your friends.

Personality Type No. 9 The Pragmatist

Pragmatists are men and women of action. When someone of this personality is present, things begin to happen. The lights come on, the music plays, the game begins. And for this type—the outstanding entrepreneur, the international diplomat, the mediator, the negotiator par excellence—a game it is.

Possible Strengths

Ability to:

- Negotiate and seek compromise to keep things moving
- Make things happen, keep things lively
- Take a realistic approach
- Notice and remember factual information
- Create an environment that is unbureaucratic and allows time for fun
- Provide for flexibility in doing the job and be responsive to the needs of the moment
- Embrace risk

Potential Weaknesses

May:

- Appear blunt and insensitive to others when acting quickly
- Rely too much on improvisation and miss the wider implications of actions
- Sacrifice follow-through to the next immediate problem
- Be in a setting that doesn't play to strengths (i.e., ideas and action, not details and follow-through)

The Prayer

Lord, help me to get from A to B, even if I have to walk over a few bodies to get there!

No.18 **Score High on the "Mistake" Question**

The Game:

Although the interviewer asks, "What mistakes have you made?" the real question is "What did you learn from the experience?"

The Strategy:

This game is played like tennis or golf. Strength comes in following through with your swing. Subscribe to the theory that "the only real mistake is making the same mistake twice."

uckminster Fuller said, "Man is a creature intended by his creator to learn primarily through making mistakes." He also said that we should give A's to those students who make the most mistakes because they're the ones who learn the most. However, schools are in the business of giving medals, degrees, and diplomas—not in recognizing mistakes.

The same is true in many other arenas. For instance, Mike Shanahan led the Denver Broncos to two consecutive Super Bowls. Shanahan was Coach of the Year and broke almost all Denver football franchise records. Yet he had been fired as head coach of the Los Angeles Raiders after compiling a record of eight wins and twelve losses. Not only was Shanahan fired from his first head-coaching job, but he was allegedly stiffed on part of his contract.

What Shanahan had learned was that the right boss, the right chemistry, are critical keys to winning, and he didn't make the same mistake again. He went on to set offensive records with the San Francisco 49ers and the Denver Broncos throughout the 1990s, while the Raiders hired four coaches and fired three of them during the same decade.

Making a mistake is like falling off a horse. If you can say, "I fell off the horse. Got back on. And rode the horse again," what you are really saying is, "I'm responsible for my own actions. I've learned from my mistakes. I don't repeat them or give up." (For a classic example, see Mickey Searles's story on page 123.)

The worst answer you can give is, "I can't remember making a mistake." Next to worst answer: "In 1986, I turned in my expense report two days late." Almost as bad: "Well, you know my strengths are my biggest weakness." The best answer is, "I blew an assignment for the company because I...and what I learned was...and how it helped me is...."

Personality Type No. 10   The Party Lover

This type radiates attractiveness, warmth, and optimism. Smooth, witty, charming, clever, articulate, and open—this describes the Party Lover, who represents about 13 percent of the population. They are great fun to be with and are the most generous of all the types. The one word that best describes this type is "performer."

Possible Strengths

Ability to:

- Accept and deal with people as they are
- Bring enthusiasm and cooperation to situations at work and home
- Present a positive image of an organization to others
- Link people and resources
- Create a lively, action-oriented, harmonious, people-intensive environment

Potential Weaknesses

May:

- Overemphasize subjective data
- Not reflect before jumping into situations
- Spend too much time socializing and neglect tasks
- Not always finish projects started
- Get bored easily
- Create mini-crises, just for the drama and excitement of resolving them

The Prayer

Lord, help me to take things more seriously, especially parties and dancing.

No. 18 Predict the "Strengths and Weaknesses" Questions

The Game

The strength question is also known as "What are you good at? Can you sell yourself?" But the smart interviewer knows that strengths, in the extreme, are almost always weaknesses.

The Strategy

Describe how your strengths will benefit the company. Describe one or two weaknesses. Whatever your answer, don't go on and on.

n terms of strengths, you might be asked to rank yourself on a scale of one to ten in different skills. You'll then be asked to explain why you rated yourself higher in one skill than another.

If you're candid—"people skills get a ten, financial skills get a four"—be prepared to explain yourself. For example, if you're strong with interpersonal skills and weak with analytical skills, you might say, "I've always done better at building teams than I have at analyzing financial statements." Then follow up by explaining how you play to your strengths: "That's why I've chosen positions that put me with people rather than spreadsheets."

You might also discuss how one of your strengths helped set a company policy or business strategy. Take the interviewer through a project—why it went to you, how you used your strengths to reach a decision, and how you worked with other teams and departments. Translate your strength into numbers wherever possible—increased sales and improved productivity, or more Web page views, or better return on investment. And focus on the big picture: "First, we looked at our strategy. Second, we decided where we wanted to end up. Third, we researched our customers. Finally, we set a profit margin that we could realistically achieve." In addition, *always* relate your strengths to the job you are applying for.

When an interviewer asks directly, "What are your weaknesses?" the question is similar to "What mistakes have you made?" and means "What are your shortcomings? What would you most like to improve? How well do you know yourself, and how honest are you willing to be?"

For example, if priorities are a serious problem you can always say, "At work, I tend to start too many projects and may have difficulty finishing them. But I've learned to complete my work, even if I have to work nights and weekends."

Don't say, "I'm a perfectionist who likes to have everything exactly right before it leaves my office. So I work long hours…." Most interviewers have heard these weaknesses-that-are-really-strengths hundreds of times, and they'll go on automatic pilot for the next half-hour and not hear a word you're saying.

What if the interviewer goes the indirect route and asks about strengths but listens for weaknesses?

Let's say you're a good team player and use phrases like "good consensus builder," "good listener," and "good feel for people" to describe yourself. Playing the Opposite Game, an experienced interviewer will wonder, "Consensus builder, eh?" Does he avoid confrontation and sweep problems under the rug? "Good listener?" Does he have trouble making hard decisions, especially about people? "A good feel for people?" Does he have an overwhelming need to be well liked?

Perceptive interviewers may also ask about your athletic interests and wonder what's on the other side of the looking glass. They realize that soccer and basketball are, for example, team sports, but rock climbing and distance running are not.

Don't overthink the strengths and weaknesses questions. Play to your strengths. But what are your strengths? What are your weaknesses? If unsure, you can always check out the personality charts of strengths and weaknesses that appear throughout the book.

Then rehearse your strengths and weaknesses *before* the interview starts. As Shakespeare said, readiness is all.

No.20 Prepare for the "Lying" Question

The Game:

The interviewer says, "Have you ever lied or cheated in your life?" How should you answer this one? If you say "No," the interviewer will believe you're lying. If you say "Yes," the interviewer will be very interested in what you say next. This may not be fair—heads, you lose; tails you lose—but this is the way the game is played.

The Strategy:

Be honest. But also be smart. As in the "Mistake" question, follow through and show what lesson(s) you learned from the experience.

**B**efore he was elected president and sent 450,000 U.S. troops to fight in Vietnam, Lyndon B. Johnson said, "We are not about to send American boys…to do what Asian boys ought to be doing for themselves."

- Before Watergate, Richard Nixon said, "I'm not a crook."
- Before his re-election campaign, George Bush said, "Read my lips. No new taxes!"
- Before his Grand Jury testimony, Bill Clinton said, while wagging his finger, "I did not have sexual relations with that woman."

So what's the big deal? Politicians lie. We've known that for years and are actually surprised when a politician tells the truth. In fact, most people, not just politicians, hide things and make misrepresentations.

According to one estimate of the Ward Howell search firm, 65 percent of executives lie about their academic credentials. Forty-three percent lie about their job responsibilities. Forty-two percent lie about their previous compensation. In addition, 80 percent of high school students in America and 70 percent of college students admit to cheating on exams. And every day newspapers run stories of people and organizations hiding things and carrying out hidden agendas.

Bill Ford, Jr., chairman of Ford Motor Company and vice-chairman of the Detroit Lions said, "I could look the chairman of General Motors or Toyota in the eye, and if they shake your hand and give you their word, it's good. Here (in the National Football League) it's not the case. There's always a hidden agenda. All I can say is, thank goodness the sport of football is still a great sport, because the business of football isn't."

Is this story typical? I think so.

I recall a candidate in Chicago who looked around the office and hesitated after I asked, "What will be the surprises when the company checks your background?" He slowly licked his lips and said, "No surprises." Of course, I didn't believe him, but I didn't know what his hidden agenda was.

It turned out that the candidate had had three drunk driving arrests as part of his official record. Although his driving history was part of the public record, he didn't think anyone would find out about the DUIs, so he had decided to stonewall in the interview. Therefore I didn't trust the fellow. Despite my recommendation, the candidate was hired and he turned out to be an unmitigated disaster.

You never know whether the interviewer, like a good trial lawyer, already knows the answer to the question he's asking you, such as "Have you ever…?" So have a well-thought-out strategy for the question "Have you ever lied before?" And if you say, "Yes, I have," give a specific example.

I have one unusual friend who was comfortable with using his personal life as an example, and he said, "I lied to my wife about XYZ because I didn't trust how she would react. She found out, and it took me several months to repair the damage. If I were in that situation again… I hope that I would…."

Would I be so honest? I doubt it.

It's one thing to omit a marital problem or even fudge on a speeding ticket, especially if you've gone to traffic school and paid your dues. But when it comes to academic credentials, job responsibilities, job compensation, or litigation history—these public records and official documents can easily be checked out—and often they will be.

If you want to know what an interviewer might find out, I'd suggest that you check out the public record—on yourself. The cost is about $100. Most records are kept at the state level, so it's best to go to your state Web site and work from there. Then you could move on to sites like the public record sites listed on page 188.

No.21 Do Lunch or Be Lunch

The Game:

"Can you join me for lunch?" This is a game encountered mostly at higher levels of management.

The Strategy:

If you want the job, say "Yes." And if you're asked, "What about dinner with our spouses or significant others?" Say "Yes" too. You should understand this game at three different levels.

**evel No. 1—Table Manners.** You're taken to an expensive restaurant with an executive who fancies himself a wine aficionado. If social graces are a part of the job—and for executives, they almost always are—and if your host asks you to order the wine, defer to the connoisseur. Don't turn to the waiter and say, "Just bring us a bottle of red." Let the connoisseur pick from the wine list.

Then there is the question of how much wine. In the hiring game, beware of employers who drink a full bottle of wine, especially at lunch. Your host will also be watching how much you consume, so I'd suggest that you avoid the wine and hard stuff. And never, ever offer to pick up the check.

Level No. 2—Client Chemistry. There's another part of the lunch game. The interviewer wonders how you'll conduct yourself with the company's clients. You may discover a client has been invited to join you at lunch, and your chemistry with him or her is what's important.

I recall a recruiter for Goldman Sachs telling me that she routinely met with five candidates at a time and talked with them for a few minutes at pre-interview cocktail parties. In those few minutes, she learned to predict quite accurately which candidates would do well with clients and which would not.

Level No. 3—Partner Chemistry. The Young Presidents' Organization (YPO) includes spouses at all chapter meetings and conferences. Significant others are, well, significant others.

So an invitation to drinks or dinner with your partner is a critical part of the hiring game. Can your partner mix with other members? What are his or her strengths and weaknesses? This filter may not be fair, but I've seen the Young Presidents' Organization admit a candidate because of his or her terrific partner, whereas the opposite is also true.

It happens in businesses as well, and you should know it.

Personality Type No. 11 The Distracted and Charismatic Type

These types have an uncanny sense of the motivations of others. This gives them a talent for seeing life as an exciting drama, pregnant with possibilities for both good and evil. This type, however, often berates itself for being so self-conscious. Only about 5 percent of the population fall into this category, but they have great influence because of their extraordinary impact on others.

Possible Strengths

Ability to:

- Focus on possibilities, especially with people
- Genuinely appreciate other people
- Motivate and energize others with their contagious enthusiasm
- Recognize new possibilities
- Supply ingenuity to problems
- Prepare for the future
- Originate projects and take action

Potential Weaknesses

May:

- Start too many projects and have difficulty finishing them
- Take criticism and other things too personally
- Get off track; become preoccupied with irrelevant tangents
- Be prone to possibly addictive behavior (eating, drinking, exercising, etc., to excess)

The Prayer

Lord, help me keep my mind on one th… LOOK, A BIRD! …ing at a time.

No.22 Expect Trick Questions

The Game:

You are given a problem to solve. "A man goes to a party and is the first to drink some punch. He leaves early. Everyone else at the party who drinks the punch later dies of poisoning. Why doesn't the man die?"

The Strategy:

The interviewer wants to see how well you think on your feet. Don't say, "I haven't the foggiest idea," or "How is this relevant to the job?" Play it straight. Personally, I hate trick questions, because I always get them wrong.

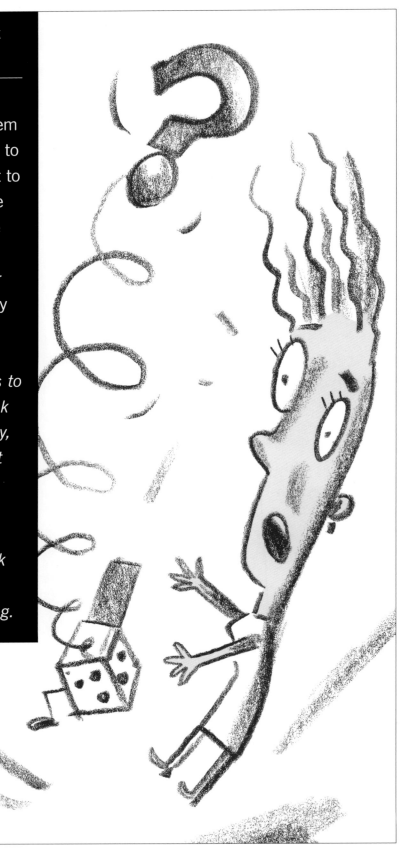

In the previous example, for instance, you could say, "Because the man poisons the punch before he leaves." Or "The poison is in the ice cubes, which haven't begun to melt before the man finishes his drink and leaves the party." Or "It was a cold night, and the heater was defective. All the guests died of carbon monoxide poisoning, except for the guest who left early." Or "The poison was in the crackers and pâté that were served to the other guests after the fellow left the party." The classic answer is "the ice cubes," but it's obvious that there can be more than one solution. The point, when you've been thrown a curveball, is to see if you can hit it.

Here's an example of a curveball question from an interviewer who is head of an ad agency in Florida.

He's taking notes during your interview and suddenly says, "Please name ten kinds of cheeses." Is he joking or serious? You answer, and the interviewer records what you've said. Next he says, "What is the average rainfall in the Amazon Basin?" You look like a deer caught in the headlights, but he couldn't care less and awaits your answer.

These crazy questions are a test of your creativity and sense of humor. After all, this is an ad agency! There are no right answers except to get the joke and play along. For the rainfall question, the perfect response would be an absolute deadpan "In inches or centimeters?"

Some people think that you can prepare for such questions, but I believe that there's no way you can prepare for trick questions because there are hundreds of them.

Here are five examples.

1. Two American coins add up to fifty-five cents.

If one of them is not a nickel, what are the two coins?

2. Make one word from the following jumbled letters:

O R E N O D W.

3. An explorer found a coin marked 7 B.C.

He was then told it was a forgery. Why?

4. Please fill in the blanks in the following sequence:

1 4 7 (?) 2 5 8 0 3 6 9 (?).

5. Why is a manhole cover round?

Answers:

1. Half dollar, nickel (one of them is not a nickel but the other is).

2. ONE WORD.

3. How could a coin have been minted seven years B.C. (Before Christ) when Christ wasn't born yet? Why would the minter put "B.C." on the coin?

4. The numbers appear to be the columns in a telephone keypad.

If so, the sequence would be: 1 4 7 * 2 5 8 0 3 6 9 #

5. So it can be rolled.

There's a variation on trick questions where interviewers describe a situation or project they're working on, and ask what kind of analysis you would do, and where you would go to get the data. To turn the situation to your advantage: Think before you speak and lay out several options for the interviewer.

The best you can do—with trick questions or situational analyses—is answer honestly, or creatively, and look on the experience as one of the more common games that companies play.

No.23 **Win the "Do You Have Any Questions?" Game**

The Game:

There are two hidden agendas behind this question.

1. Have you researched the company?

2. What are your concerns about the position?

The Strategy:

The "Any questions?" game is like the two-minute warning in a football game. With the two-minute warning, rules change, and so should your game plan. Take this opportunity to show that you've done your homework.

I t's always amazing to me that candidates are so poorly prepared to deal with "Is there anything I haven't asked?" or "What would you like to ask me?"

A graduate student was interviewing with the National Basketball Association (NBA) for one of four international marketing positions. The NBA gets about 1,000 applications per week. For his final interview, the applicant traveled to Atlanta to attend a marketing expo and have an interview with Commissioner David Stern.

The applicant had watched David Stern being interviewed on *Meet the Press* the previous Sunday. So when Commissioner Stern said, "You have time for only one question," the candidate was prepared. "Were there any surprises on *Meet the Press*?" David Stern never answered the question, but the "one shot" was offbeat, and the commissioner knew it. The student got the job.

My wife interviews hundreds of high school kids for summer scholarships. She usually has a specific read on each student within ten minutes. However, if she's still unsure about a youngster, at the end of the interview, she asks one final question, "Do you have any questions for me?"

The students almost always pause—they're extremely nervous—and if they come back with a question, almost any question, they're in the program. If they say, "Not really"— they're not candidates for the scholarship.

In my psychiatric practice, I always announced to

patients that we had five more minutes. It was a flashing yellow light—speed up or slow down—because your hour is almost up. That's when a person invariably said, "Oh, one more thing…" or "I almost forgot…" and it would turn out to be the most important thing that person had to tell me.

I advise you to pay attention when an interviewer asks, "Do you have any questions?" at the end of an interview. It may be the most important question you're asked.

The best answer you can give is, "Yes," while you pull out a typed sheet of ten to fifteen questions. However, don't ask, "What's your vision for the company?"—it's too predictable. Instead, I'd ask an unpredictable question, such as "What emerging markets do you see for your company in the next five years, and what are the pros and cons of each market?"

Then go down the list of written questions you've prepared. Tick off the ones the interviewer has already answered and start going through the rest. Your preparation will make a lasting impression on most interviewers.

If every last question has already been answered, look the interviewer in the eye and tell him how interesting it was to visit. You'd like to think about everything you've learned and get back to him. Then do it. Send a list of questions by fax or e-mail the following day.

Personality Type No. 12

This type wishes to exercise its ingenuity in the world of people and things. This type is good at analysis and has both a tolerance for, and enjoyment of, the complex. Usually enthusiastic, they are apt to express interest in everything, and thus are a source of inspiration to others. They are also delighted over many things and are relatively easy to please.

Possible Strengths

Ability to:

- Be flexible and spontaneous
- Tackle new problems with zest
- View limitations as challenges to be overcome
- Provide ingenuity to problems
- Enjoy complex challenges
- Reward risk-taking
- Encourage autonomy

Potential Weaknesses

May:

- Become lost in the future model, forgetting about present realities
- Be competitive and unappreciative of the input of others
- Overextend themselves
- Start too many projects and have difficulty finishing them
- Not adapt well to standard procedures
- Be prone to addictive behavior (eating, drinking, exercising, etc., to excess)

The Prayer

Lord, help me follow established procedures today. On second thought, I'll settle for a few minutes.

No.24 **Salvage a Bad Interview**

The Game:

You've left the interview with that sinking feeling— you know exactly what you did wrong. What can you do to put yourself back in the running for a job you really want?

The Strategy:

First, reread the "Mistake" Question on page 98, and then contact the interviewer. Provide an explanation of what went wrong and why— and ask for another interview. Turn the mistake to your advantage.

ast year my daughter Sara came out of an audition and realized on the way home that she'd made a mistake. She turned around, went back to the audition, and apologized to the casting agent, saying, "I should have been more vulnerable in that role." Although Sara had to wait another two hours, she did the scene again. No, she didn't get the part, but she demonstrated to the casting agent a quality far more than the role required —the ability to evaluate her own performance critically. And Sara's story is similar to one told me by Milo Shelly, who for seventeen years headed the Human Resources department at the Ernest & Julio Gallo Winery.

A fraternity brother of Milo's—Mickey Searles—was a lousy student (.8 GPA his first semester), but he had a great personality and near-Hollywood good looks. Several years ago, Mickey had interviewed with Charles Lazarus, the legendary founder or Toys "R" Us and visionary behind the concept of Kids "R" Us.

At the time, Mickey was thirty-five years old and the president of a chain of department stores based in White Plains, New York. His goal was to become a top executive in a major department store chain, so he was not particularly impressed when an executive recruiter told him about a job heading a new specialty retailer devoted to children's clothing. But he went anyway.

The interview was both good and bad. Good, because the interview was "electric." Bad, because Mickey Searles admitted to Charles Lazarus that he had never even been in any Kids "R" Us store, and Mr. Lazarus abruptly ended the conversation.

"I went home and told my wife I had just blown the opportunity of a lifetime," Mr. Searles said. Nevertheless, he wrote a letter to Mr. Lazarus saying he had made a mistake. "I told him that if we ever met again, I would know more about his stores than he did."

Taking his persistence and honesty as a good sign, Charles Lazarus did meet with Mickey Searles again and the interview was a great success. This time Mr. Searles was prepared. He went on to become president of Kids "R" Us.

Personality Type No. 13 The Administrator

The Administrator is usually a pillar of strength. The best adjective to describe this type would be "responsible." They are always so in tune with the established, time-honored institutions and ways of behaving within those institutions that they cannot understand those who might wish to abandon or radically change those institutions. They follow routines well at home and work, tending to have a place for everything and wanting everything in its place.

Possible Strengths

Ability to:

- Follow through in a step-by-step way
- Provide stability and predictability
- Be an excellent administrator
- Take charge
- Hold consistently to policies
- Be good at logical analysis
- Be good at weighing "the evidence and the law"
- Stand firm against opposition
- Produce work on time in an orderly fashion
- Monitor to see if the job is done

Potential Weaknesses

May:

- Stand too firm after making a decision; i.e., become stubborn
- Have trouble seeing and appreciating innovative alternatives
- Have trouble appreciating others' feelings
- Keep feelings in check but, paradoxically, have emotional outbursts
- Be hypersensitive to criticism
- Be less effective in freewheeling, rapidly changing situations

The Prayer

Lord, help me to try not to RUN everything. But, if You need some help, just ask!

Strategies After
the Interview

"We don't like their sound, and guitar music is on the way out."

**D**uring the Los Angeles Olympic Games, I watched the start of the women's marathon at Santa Monica City College. Little did I know that almost three hours later, a 39-year-old Swiss runner, Gabriela Andersen-Scheiss, would capture the imagination of millions of TV viewers, as well as the stadium crowd of 70,000 fans, as she entered the Los Angeles Coliseum.

Andersen-Scheiss had 500 meters to go. She been running for twenty minutes longer than the winner, Joan Benoit, and she was lurching and reeling, clearly suffering from heat exhaustion. The sun was hot, Andersen-Scheiss was severely dehydrated, and the race officials had an agonizing choice. Should they help her off the track? Should they let her stagger toward the finish line and imperil her health? Or should they repeat what officials had done in the 1908 men's marathon, helping Dorando Pietri of Italy across the finish line and in the process disqualifying him from winning the gold medal?

With 70,000 fans urging Andersen-Scheiss on, she veered away as medical officers approached her. Aware of their presence, she continued her walk-run to cover the final quarter mile. It took five minutes. But Gabriela completed the race, collapsing into the arms of the waiting doctors at the finish line.

The standing ovation she received was thunderous. It was even louder than it had been for the winner.

"Anything that is completed is beautiful," said aeronautical engineer Paul MacCready. "And if it's not completed, it isn't very good at all."

I agree, and if you want the job, completion is an important part of the process. If you stop your efforts after you leave the interviewer's office, you're missing a tremendous opportunity, as the next six strategies show.

Write a Thank-You Note

Most interviewees know to follow up any specific requests by an interviewer. There's one more thing you should always do, which is often forgotten: Say thank you.

You're under the microscope until you have an offer in hand. This is your opportunity to give yourself a slight edge. Take advantage of it. A simple thank-you note may help differentiate you from the competition.

 poll by the staffing service Accountemps found that just over a third of candidates send thank-you notes. Yet 76 percent of executives consider a thank-you note of value. So when you don't write, that's what's often remembered. Some people prefer hand-written notes; others prefer e-mail; while still others don't care as long as you promptly send a note.

When you do write, never use nicknames. Even if you were introduced to "Kenny" Hahn, it's Mr. Kenneth Hahn. Don't begin your note "Dear Kenny." And details do count. It's F. Warren Hellman not Warren F. Hellman, so if you're unsure of a name, ask for an interviewer's business card. For example, here is the beginning of a thank-you letter I received from Michael Moore, the recruiting manager for Restoration Hardware: "Dear Dr. Mornell. Thank you for seeing me on Monday. I thoroughly enjoyed our time together. Deliberately withholding from traditional Irish hyperbole, I was genuinely impressed with the questions you asked, the insight you showed, the compassion you displayed. It's my initial impression that we have more in common that our lingering fondness for our dearly departed four-legged friends."

Another candidate wrote, "It was a pleasure meeting you on Monday. Enclosed you will find some of the material we discussed. Hope this helps. Again, many thanks."

Do you prefer Irish exuberance or Puritan restraint? It's your call—whatever suits your style is the right answer.

No.26 Pay Attention to Details

The Game:

Before, during, and after the interview—most organizations want to know whether you're a detail-oriented person.

The Strategy:

Details can make or break your candidacy.

Jim Ansara tells a great story about the value of taking care of details. "[W]e got a $22-million job building an office in a large Boston high-rise—the biggest job we'd ever done. We built eleven floors in five months. We killed ourselves. And it went flawlessly. But weeks after the job was finished, we got a call from the client that a senior partner's doorknob wasn't working. In fact, he'd gotten locked in his office more than once. We went back to fix it several times, but we never did what we should have done: just taken the doorknob out and sprung for a new one. About the same time, this client was looking to build a new $8-million to $10-million building in the suburbs. And we lost that business.

"We didn't, in reality, lose it because of a doorknob. But I developed some company lessons around that story. The high-rise was one of our biggest successes and we gave great service, but we didn't achieve the level of client satisfaction we needed on the added stuff at the end. And if we had done that, maybe we would've gotten the new construction. Now I have a plaque in my office with a doorknob on it that says, 'The $8-Million Doorknob.'"

Don't blow it by overlooking the details. What counts are the little things over which you have control.

Let's say that your resume is perfect. You ace the phone call. Although your interview is rescheduled two times, you are incredibly accommodating and make the interviewer's life easier. Then you nail the interview. You impress the client who shows up for lunch, and with this client, you help conclude a deal the company had been working on for four months. Your references check out. They give specific examples of projects you've spearheaded and personal obstacles you've overcome. You follow up with a personal thank-you note.

But what if the chief operating officer of the company talks with all hires as a matter of principle, and one of his pet peeves is candidates who don't promptly return his phone calls. And you fall into that category. You're toast. Sure you might still get the job, but only if you have a champion within the company who goes to bat for you.

Like the doorknob, the prompt callback may be one of a hundred silly details, but it might just be the detail that breaks the deal—or seals it.

Personality Type No. 14 The World's Host and Hostess

The most sociable of all types, the World's Hosts and Hostesses are energized by interactions with people, tending to idealize whatever or whoever they admire. Harmony is a key to this type, which is represented in about 13 percent of the population. This type is also a great nurturer of established institutions such as the home, church, temple, school, and neighborhood groups. They are outstanding hosts and hostesses, able to call people by name, usually after one introduction.

Possible Strengths

Ability to:

- Be organized and friendly, able to voice appreciation of other people
- Work well with others, especially on teams
- Handle day-to-day operations
- Deal efficiently with crises
- Create an environment at work and home that is happy, harmonious, and relatively conflict free

Potential Weaknesses

May:

- Avoid conflict and sweep problems under the rug
- Not value own priorities because of a desire to please other people
- Not always step back and see the big picture
- Be overly sensitive, taking things too personally

The Prayer

LORD, GIVE ME PATIENCE, AND I MEAN RIGHT NOW!

No.27 Talk to Your References

The Game:

If interested, a company will check on your track record, asking for the names of your references.

The Strategy:

What more can you do? Make sure you've covered your bases with references prior to final discussions with the company.

I n *Hiring Smart*, I advise organizations to check references, and I suggest some specific strategies for doing so. For example, the company calls the names on your list in hopes of reaching their voice mail. Early in the morning. Late at night. During the lunch hour. The caller leaves a simple message. "Mollie Malone has given your name as a reference. Please call me back if she was outstanding."

If Mollie is (was) outstanding, I guarantee that four out of five of her references will want to help and call back almost immediately. On the other hand, if four out of five of her references don't call back—no confidences have been broken; no laws have been violated, but four out of five of Mollie's references have made a strong statement for the prospective employer to think about.

A friend used this technique recently. She was told by a candidate that he needed an offer within twenty-four hours because he had to make a decision, and she believed him. Calling his references my friend said, "Please call me back within two hours if the candidate is outstanding." Within two hours, all five references had called her back, and she hired the candidate that day.

If you're a finalist, good interviewers will check your references, and good companies—ones you want to work for—will definitely check on you officially and unofficially. By "unofficially," I mean that an experienced interviewer may very likely discount your official list of references and discreetly check you out without your permission, especially for high-level positions.

Therefore, especially if you haven't gotten along with a boss or co-worker, it's always best to be relatively honest. You don't want a reference giving you the following types of recommendations, which were taken from actual employee performance evaluations:

"Since my last report, this employee has reached rock bottom and has started to dig."

"His men would follow him anywhere, but only out of morbid curiosity."

"I would not allow this employee to breed."

"Works well when under constant supervision and cornered like a rat in a trap."

"When she opens her mouth, it seems that this is only to change whichever foot was previously in there."

"He would be out of his depth in a parking lot puddle."

"This young lady has delusions of adequacy."

"He sets low personal standards and then consistently fails to achieve them."

"This employee is depriving a village somewhere of an idiot."

"This employee should go far—and the sooner he starts, the better."

References
Top Ten List

1. Provide references only upon request
   or if you're a finalist.

2. Start with three to six references,
   if you have them.

3. Pick people who know you well from work—
   superiors, peers, and subordinates.

4. Ask them if they'll be a reference.

5. Ask them what they'll say.
   (They may or may not be candid.)

6. Ask *where* they prefer to be contacted.

7. Ask *when* they prefer to be contacted.

8. Get an e-mail address if they prefer an
   electronic request.

9. Call your references *before* they'll be
   contacted by an employer.

10. Call your references *after* a decision
   is made to thank them for their help.

No.28 Propose a Tryout Period

The Game:

If an organization gives a green light, that's great. If it's a red light, it's not so great. But what if you get a flashing yellow? How do you proceed with caution and influence the hiring decision?

The Strategy:

Offer to work for three hours, or three days, with the interviewing company. Your goal is to demonstrate your strengths under game conditions and to show you can perform under pressure.

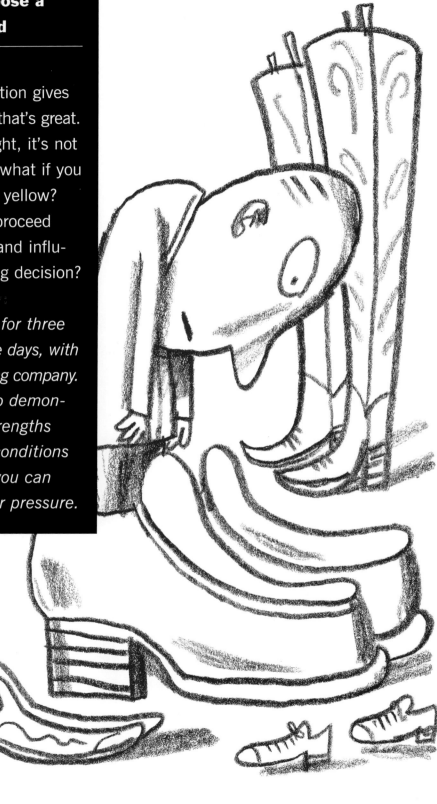

I work in Mill Valley, California. A community of 9,000, Mill Valley has six coffee shops within a four-block radius of downtown, but only one coffee shop opens at 6 a.m. Since I'm an early morning person, I went into that shop, ordered a coffee, and the fellow behind the counter introduced himself.

"Hi, I'm Carroll."

"How do you spell your name?"

"C-A-R-R-O-L-L," he said. "But, everyone calls me 'Cal.' It's also what my wife calls me." He smiled and said, "Ah, correction—my estranged wife."

We both laughed. "My name is Pierre," I replied, and after I got my coffee, Cal left me alone to read the morning paper.

Paying my bill fifteen minutes later, I said goodbye to Cal.

"Goodbye, Pierre," he said. "Thanks for coming in."

According to Dale Carnegie, the most important word in the English language is our name, and Cal had remembered my name. So out of the six coffee shops in downtown Mill Valley, which do you think I'll remember the next time around?

Could I have predicted Cal's good memory and people skills from an interview? Maybe. But if I had seen Cal in action over, say, a three-hour or three-day shift, could I have seen his memory and talent in action? Yes. And what has Cal got to lose by working a temporary shift if he's considering the job?

Here's another example.

My youngest daughter, Mara, worked in Australia for

two years on the *Sydney Weekly* after her college graduation. Returning to America, Mara bound her eighty-five newspaper articles into an oversized red binder. But looking at her portfolio, most editors laughed at her limited experience, and she was rejected for jobs on small newspapers in Santa Barbara, San Diego, Norfolk, Groton, and Boston.

One San Francisco TV "personality" scanned her portfolio and suggested that Mara go to Medford, Oregon, where she could work as an assistant producer. "After three years in Medford," Ms. TV said sarcastically, "you could probably move up to Portland."

After four months of rejections, Mara went to New York City where she offered to work in the mailroom and carry coffee part-time at a New York daily newspaper. Four years later, at age 26, she became the youngest editor ever on that paper, the *New York Post*.

This policy works for most jobs.

A good friend of mine visited construction sites during his college summers. He offered to work as a carpenter gratis for a week. If the head carpenter liked his work—fine—he could employ my friend and pay him for the previous week. If not, he'd be on his way without receiving any compensation.

He was always hired.

Note: I'm told by an employment attorney that when there's a question about the status of the employment relationship, workers' compensation benefits may not apply.

Here is how one candidate, Ben Balbale, performed under game conditions. As part of a summer internship at Siebel Systems, he was given an interactive project to complete. At the top of the page, Ben listed dates and locations, and in the left column, he itemized activities to be covered. The bar graphs represent his time lines for getting the job done. Of all the summer interns, Ben was the only candidate to be offered a permanent job.

Siebel Interactive Summer Project Plan	Location											
Draft	MA					CA				MA		
Objective / Activity	May 25	Jun 1	Jun 8	Jun 15	Jun 22	Jun 29	Jul 8	Jul 13	Jul 20	Jul 27	Aug 3	Aug 10
1. Project Ramp-up	▄											
1.1 Finalize Project Plan												
1.2 Collect Siebel contact information for CPG/Pharma												
2. Complete Business Plan One (assuming 50% completion)	▄▄▄											
2.1 Collect Siebel feedback on developed strategy												
2.3 Confirm data sources and information providers												
2.4 Evaluate current licensing/revenue model												
3. Develop Business Plan for Industry One and Two												
3.1 Contact Siebel Sales, PM, set up meetings		▄										
3.2 Meet with Siebel Sales, PM's in Verticals				▄▄								
3.3 Size the market, collect external data					▄▄▄							
3.4 Select client interview list/set up customer visits					▄							
3.5 Conduct customer visits						▄▄						
3.6 Develop marketing plan, collecting feedback,								▄▄				
and integrating plan with Siebel marketing plans									▄▄			
3.7 Contact information providers in industry										▄▄		
3.8 Create draft licensing agreements										▄▄		
3.9 Write Business Plans												
4. Develop Prototypes												
4.1 Work with technical team to create specs						▄▄						
4.2 Create static prototypes							▄▄					
4.3 Collect Siebel feedback on prototypes from Siebel team									▄▄			
4.4 Collect Siebel feedback from selected customers									▄▄			
4.5 Incorporate feedback										▄▄		
5. Present to Siebel Exec Team												▄
6. Project Wrap-up and Handoff												▄

No.29 **Negotiate the Offer—Top Eight List**

The Game:

You've almost achieved your objective, and you're in the negotiating stage. You want a signing bonus. The company wants to give you a bonus after a year. Now what?

The Strategy:

Know those negotiating factors over which you have control and those over which you have no control.

Four terrific books on negotiations are listed on page 190. However, here's my top eight list for negotiating an offer.

1. Establish a relationship. The more time you spend with a person, the more effort they'll usually spend negotiating with you.

2. Know the facts. What's the range of comparable salaries in comparable jobs in comparable industries?

3. Figure out what your "dream" package is. If the genie came out of the bottle, what would you ask for? What is reasonable compensation for the work you'll be doing? Are you looking for salary? Bonus? Car allowance? Vacation? Deferred compensation? Stock options? If there are peculiarities to your package, you may want to let the company know: "I have to be on such-and-such health plan to cover my family member's preexisting condition," or "I'm in the Army Reserve and will need to take this amount of time each year for that commitment." Defining these parameters will make your decision easier when you receive the offer.

4. Know if the offer is negotiable. Most people are responsive to expressed concerns and proposed solutions. They're rarely responsive to pressure for more money if it isn't backed by a thoughtful argument. Make sure you know what you want, and be clear about the reasons for it. "I would love to work here, but I just can't cover my mortgage on that salary."

5. **Ask about internal candidates.** Were there any people considered internally? Who are they? Are they staying? Find out their strengths and interests. These people can be your greatest allies—they've given thought to the job and the organization—but they could also be your greatest critics. If they feel slighted by your appointment, they may be eager to see you fail. Discuss with the management what measures will be taken to develop a relationship with these people. What is being done to keep them engaged, productive, happy? What will be done should issues arise?

6. **If you take a lower offer, ask for a six-month review instead of a one-year review.** If the employer isn't willing to evaluate you in 180 days, rethink the offer.

7. **If you take the higher offer, understand the reasons for it.** Have you been swayed by the money? Or is it just that the company doesn't want to lose you to someone else?

8. **Be prepared to walk away from the offer.** The ability to "walk away" is a trump card used by every successful negotiator that I know of.

Personality Type No. 15 The Honey-Tongued Orator

These types are outstanding leaders. They have the charming characteristic of seeming to take for granted that they will be followed, never doubting that people will want to do what they suggest. And, more often than not, people do follow, because this type has unusual charisma. These types place a high value on cooperation from others and are most willing to cooperate themselves. They make very good politicians.

Possible Strengths

Ability to:

- Enjoy leading and facilitating teams
- Encourage cooperation
- Bring strong ideals of how organizations should treat people
- Communicate organizational values
- Bring matters to fruitful conclusions
- Focus on changing things for the betterment of others
- Be supportive and social
- Have a spirit of harmony

Potential Weaknesses

May:

- Idealize others and suffer from blind loyalty
- Sweep problems under the rug when faced with conflict
- Avoid confrontation and conflict
- Ignore the task in favor of relationship issues
- Take criticism personally

The Prayer

Lord, help me to do only what I can, and trust You for the rest. Also, Lord, you don't mind if I lead the parade, do you?

No.30 Pick Your Best Strategies

The Game:
This isn't a game, it's reality.

The Strategy:
In every game I know of—from checkers to chess, tennis to golf, politics to business, Doom to Quake—each player finds a style that suits them, and so should you.

t the end of every speech, I always ask the audience, "What tip(s) can you use tomorrow? What are your best take-home ideas?" If there are 100 people in the audience, there will usually be ninety-five different answers that reflect the diversity of the group.

From the Summary Chart for *Games Companies Play* on pages 161–171 choose three or more strategies that best fit your situation. Use them the next time you're a job hunter. If they work, great. If not, for whatever reason, pick another three strategies and try again.

Your favorite strategies:

1.

2.

3.

4.

5.

Other strategies that will work:

1. _____

_____

2. _____

_____

3. _____

_____

Strategies that won't work:

1. _____

_____

2. _____

_____

3. _____

_____

Personality Type No. 16 — The Natural Leader

If one word were used to capture this type's style, it would be "commandant." The basic driving force and need are to lead, and from an early age they can be observed taking over groups. Their unique personalities give them a very high need for control. The entire world seems like a chessboard, with pieces in need of being moved—by them—for the greater good.

Possible Strengths

Ability to:

- Be a charismatic, strong leader people look to for direction
- Have a creative vision and clearly communicate it
- Think strategically
- Work on ideas with ingenuity and logic
- Take charge in crises
- Hold consistently to a plan
- Stand firm against opposition

Potential Weaknesses

May:

- Be too controlling, domineering, and impatient
- Meddle in others' business
- Be hypersensitive; take criticism too personally
- Overlook people's needs in focusing on bottom-line results
- Ignore and repress feelings
- Paradoxically, have strong emotional outbursts and unpredictable and inappropriate rages
- Overlook the details, practical considerations, and pitfalls in visionary thinking

The Prayer

Lord, help me to slow downandnotrushthrough whatIdoandnotbesucha controlfreak! Amen!!

Conclusion

"The concept is interesting and well-formed, but in order to earn better than a 'C,' the idea must be feasible."

**W**hy is the hiring of good people so important, especially today? One reason is the changing face of America. Ed Michaels, who helped manage the McKinsey study called "The War for Talent," put it this way:

"A lot of it has to do with demographics. In fifteen years, there will be 15 percent fewer Americans in the thirty-five- to forty-five-year-old range than there are now. At the same time, the U.S. economy is likely to grow at a rate of 3 percent to 4 percent per year. So over that period, the demand for bright, talented thirty-five- to forty-five-year-olds will increase by, say, 25 percent, and the supply will be going down by 15 percent. That sets the stage for a talent war."

That's what's going on today—the Great Talent War—and it's good news for you, the job hunter, because it's now up to you to distinguish yourself as a talent and seal the deal.

Several years ago John Nabor and I spoke at a conference, and he gave a speech that I'll never forget. John was a world-class swimmer out of the University of Southern California. He told about looking at Olympic records and realizing that he'd have to take four seconds off his time for the backstroke to compete for a medal. Since there was no way he could do that, he almost gave up. Then John realized that he had four years to train, which meant a one-second-per-year improvement, which he still couldn't imagine. Then he realized that he swam 365 days a year.

"Four years before the Games," John later told a reporter, "I knew that I had to improve 1/365th of a second each day—that's less than the blink of an eye—and I could visualize that."

John Nabor practiced his way to success one day at a time, getting a tiny bit better every day. At the Montreal Olympic Games, he won four golds and one silver medal.

Is it worth 1/365th of a second per day to win an Olympic medal? That's your call. But is it worth the time and effort to get the job you want? I think it is.

Whether it's 1/365th of a second, or one step at a time, the key to any success—personal or professional—begins and ends with your preparation, effort, and desire to win. If you reach for the stars instead of setting your sights on the foothills, you're more likely to hit the top of the mountain. You've got to be willing to go for the summit. Or, as Ralph Waldo Emerson put it: "What lies behind us and what lies ahead of us are small matters compared to what lies within us."

One final note. The strategies in this book evolved with the invaluable input of many people, and I hope that I'll hear more from readers. I'm particularly interested in ways that you have distinguished yourself that have not been mentioned in the book. Send your thoughts to me at my e-mail address, pmornell@aol.com, or to One Park Avenue, Mill Valley, CA 94941.

Many thanks, and good luck.

"If you don't paddle your own canoe, you don't move."

—Katharine Hepburn, Academy Award winner

Summary Chart for Games Companies Play

In the previous pages, I've suggested a list of practical ways for winning the hiring games companies play. As you cannot build a house by blueprints alone, you cannot do any job without the right tools. Use this Summary Chart as a toolbox that you can pick up at your own discretion.

Game	Strategy
1. Do Your Homework	
Good interviewers will know immediately if you're familiar with their organization. If you're not, regardless of what they say, they'll probably see a flashing red light.	Whether you're applying for a $25,000 or $250,000 position, a little pre-interview research goes a long way. No interviewer will fail to be impressed that your interest has a genuine foundation. Besides, in doing your homework, you might even rule out the job!
2. Network, Network, Network	
Most companies look for candidates everywhere and anywhere.	Talk to anyone and everyone you know inside and outside the organization. The best jobs are rarely advertised.
3. Master E-Mail	
You get an e-mail or you're asked to check out the organization's Web site.	Consider e-mail requests an opportunity to demonstrate your skills, interest, responsiveness, and problem-solving abilities.

Game	Strategy
4. Write the Perfect Resume	
In order to narrow the possibilities, it's common for a company to make some very basic choices from the moment your resume is submitted. Companies look for reasons to put your resume in one of three piles—A, B, or C.	In most cases you can't ensure yourself a spot in Pile A—but you can keep yourself out of Pile C.
5. Personalize Your Cover Letter	
The company asks you for a one-page cover letter that describes your interest in the job. Do you care enough to personalize your response? Are there typos in your letter? Are you literate or illiterate? Organized or sloppy? How long does it take for you to send the cover letter by mail or fax?	Respond quickly. No typos. This is a great opportunity to establish your compelling interest in the job.

Game	Strategy
6. Prepare for an Initial Phone Call	
Before you meet, the interviewer calls you to request extra copies of your resume or confirm the time of your appointment. What was that all about? The interviewer wants to know how easy it is to reach you. If she gets your voice mail, she wants to hear the kind of message you've left for callers.	Unless you are doing cartoon voice-overs for Disney, goofball messages are an absolute no-no. Your voice-mail message should be professional and to the point. No cute stuff.
7. Expect Changes in Interview Schedules	
Companies sometimes change interview arrangements because of "scheduling problems."	Regardless, be flexible. Respond quickly. Don't give the company reasons to get rid of you.
8. Start with the Receptionist	
Smart companies notice your interaction with everyone— including assistants, secretaries, and receptionists.	Waiting rooms are often where an interview starts. Pay close attention to all office personnel you meet, no matter how junior.

Game	Strategy
9. Observe the Clues in Front of You	
Many interviewers will start selling the organization as soon as the right candidate sits down.	When you buy a used car, you don't just listen to the salesman. You look at the car, kick the tires, and make your own assessment before taking a test drive. Notice the clues before the interview starts.
10. Know That Most Companies Have Biases	
A company knows the key to the future is a diverse workforce. Does it put its money where its mouth is, or are its interviewers still inclined to hire people just like themselves?	It's your call as to whether this is a deal maker or deal breaker. If you have concerns but really want the job, it may not help your cause to ask, "Mr. Jones, what is being done to change your company's culture to make it more sensitive to diversity?"

Game	Strategy
11. Have Your Pitch Down Pat: The Three Basic Rules	
You've passed the first two or ten hurdles, but the company is still looking for ways to disqualify you. There are people before you and after you who are selling themselves to the organization. It's your task to rise above the competition and seize the day.	Give the interviewers more than they expect. Establish that you would be a good fit for the company. Above all, project energy, enthusiasm, and personality. No one wants to work with boring people.
12. Read the Interviewer's Style	
Most interviewers find a technique that suits them and stick with it.	Read the interviewer's style accurately. Watch for changes in pace or sentence structure. Think of this as a game of chess and base your reactions on the interviewer's actions.
13. Trust Your Instincts	
Many interviewers pay attention to their gut instinct. How they feel about you in the first minutes will often determine how they play the rest of the interview.	Note your gut reaction, too. Is this a place you would want to spend ten hours a day for the next two, three, or ten years?

Game	Strategy
14. Recognize the Human Resources Game	
When you're asked to call Human Resources, it's a little like playing Monopoly and coming up with the card that says "Go directly to jail. Do not pass Go. Do not collect $200." Why? Because most HR departments are looking for ways to *dis*qualify you.	If you're thoughtful, direct, and ask good questions—"How do you plan to continue the 20 percent growth mentioned in your annual report? What will be the resistance?"—most interviewers are going to have trouble screening you out.
15. Understand the Real Question(s)	
A good trial lawyer will tell a client before a court appearance, "Ask yourself, 'What's behind the other attorney's question?' Then gear your answers to avoid the other attorney's traps."	Your job is to understand what, if anything, is behind commonly asked questions and to address the interviewers *real* concerns in your answers.
16. Discover the Real Problem(s)	
An organization's stated problem is rarely the real problem that it faces. Like the Cautionary Tale, what you see is often not what you get.	Your job is to identify the underlying problem and help the person who has it.

Game	Strategy
17. Predict the "Tell Me About Yourself" Question	
The real question is "Tell me something I can't get from your resume or references."	Before you go to the interview, know what you want to pitch. Then pitch away. Always tell the interviewer more than what's in your resume.
18. Score High on the "Mistake" Question	
Most hirers are skeptical of candidates who don't admit to making mistakes and learning from the experience. They want to know if you're the type who takes responsibility or blames others for your errors.	Subscribe to the theory "The only real mistake is making the same mistake twice." Be specific. Give an example. You should also follow through by emphasizing how a mistake has improved your performance.
19. Predict the "Strengths and Weaknesses" Questions	
The strength question is also known as, "What are you good at? Can you sell yourself?" This question serves another purpose since a smart interviewer is well aware that strengths, in the extreme, often predict weaknesses.	You will be asked this question. Cite your strengths and weaknesses. Don't go on and on. This is where your homework will pay off. Know the answer cold.

Game	Strategy
20. Prepare for the "Lying" Question	
The interviewer asks, "Have you ever lied or cheated in your life?" How should you answer this one? If you say "no," the interviewer will believe you're lying. If you say "yes," the interviewer will be very interested in what you say next.	Be honest. But also be smart. When you are asked the unanswerable, someone is trying to see how well you think on your feet. Answer creatively and logically, and know that there are few incorrect answers, other than no answer at all.
21. Do Lunch or Be Lunch	
"Can you join me for lunch?" is the question. "Yes" is the answer. This is a game encountered mostly at higher levels of management.	You should understand this game at three different levels: 1) table manners, 2) client chemistry, and 3) partner chemistry. All may be important.
22. Expect Trick Questions	
The interviewer gives you a trick question or a project the company is working on. How will you solve it?	The interviewer wants to know how you analyze problems. I'd suggest that you 1) think before you speak, and 2) offer several options.

Game	Strategy
23. Win the "Do You Have Any Questions?" Game	
This may be the most important question you're asked in the interview. It's crucial to do your homework and make a list of questions *before* the interview starts.	Make a list of ten questions before the interview. Cross off the ones the interviewer has already answered and ask the rest.
24. Salvage a Bad Interview	
You can almost feel the interviewer crossing your name off the list and tossing your resume into the wastebasket. What can you do to put yourself back in the running for a job you really want?	First, reread "Score High on the 'Mistake' Question" on page 98, and then contact the interviewer. Provide an explanation of what went wrong and why, and ask for another interview.
25. Write a Thank-You Note	
How do you clinch a new potential business relationship?	You're under the microscope until you have an offer in hand. This is your opportunity to give yourself a slight edge. Take advantage of it. A simple thank-you note may help differentiate you from the competition.

Game	Strategy
26. Pay Attention to Details	
Before, during, and after the interview—most organizations want to know whether you are a detail-oriented person.	Don't blow the assignment— or the work you've put into the interview process—by overlooking the details. What counts are the little things over which you have control.
27. Talk to Your References	
If interested, a company will check on your track record, usually asking for the names of your references if you are a finalist.	What else can you do? Give interviewers a sense of what they'll hear and prepare your references for the call.
28. Propose a Tryout Period	
The company tells you you're in the running, but you get the feeling you're not the top candidate.	If an organization gives a yellow light, offer to work for three, thirty, or ninety days on a temporary basis. This is a particularly good strategy for the under experienced candidate.

Game	Strategy
29. Negotiate the Offer	
You've almost achieved your objective, and you're in the negotiating stage. You want a signing bonus. The company wants to give you a bonus after a year. Now what?	Some negotiating steps are in your control, some aren't. Your job is to know the difference.
30. Pick Your Best Strategies	
This isn't a game—it's reality.	Look over the previous twenty-nine strategies. Pick out your favorite ideas and use these tips next time you're in the job market.

"If we don't get the people thing right, we lose; it is the most important thing in all our businesses."

End Games

This section answers the questions, What are some questions that I should prepare for in advance of an interview? What are examples of curveball questions and answers? What are the legal considerations? And are there any more games companies play? (There are.) This section is followed by a resource guide of Internet job sources and excellent books that you may also find helpful.

Forty Interview Questions

- What questions do you have for me? (If asked first, the question really means "Have you researched the company?")
- What will your former employer say about you—positive and negative?
- What will your former subordinates say about you?
- How do you recognize incompetence? What do you do about it?
- How do you recognize excellence? What do you do about it?
- What about yourself would you most like to improve?
- What makes you lose your temper? Tell me about the last time it happened.
- Why are you leaving (did you leave) your current job?

- Tell me about your strengths. Tell me about your weaknesses.
- What are (were) your boss's strengths and weaknesses?
- How do you plan to leave your current job? Be specific.
- What can your current employer do to keep you?
- What is your biggest fear of the new job?
- We will do a thorough background check— what will be the surprises?
- On a 1-to-10 scale—with 10 the highest— how do you rate your skills?
- How are you going to lose money for me? (Where have you made mistakes before? Where might you make mistakes again?)
- Tell me about yourself.
- Tell me about a recent failure. What did you learn?
- Why have you held so many jobs? Why have you held so few jobs?
- Why do you want to work for us?
- How will we measure your performance?
- How many people have you hired/promoted/fired? Give me an example of each.
- What are your salary expectations?
- Why should we hire you?
- What motivates you? How do you motivate people?
- Why are you in the job market?

- What are the best and worst aspects of your current position?
- How do you resolve conflict?
- Have you ever gone out on a limb on a job? Tell me what happened.
- What is the biggest mistake you have made in your career?
- Describe your current organization chart and how you fit into it.
- Have you ever been terminated from a job? Why?
- What actions do you take before you terminate an employee?
- Describe your ideal work environment.
- Have you ever made an unpopular management decision? What happened?
- What is the biggest decision you ever had to make?
- Tell me a joke.
- Tell me something I won't hear from any of your references.
- What's your impression of me?
- What would you do if you won the lottery?

Ten Questions Asked of Top Management Candidates

- What are the company's revenues per employee?

- How do the figures compare with the competition's?

- What are the revenue-per-employee figures for each of the company's leading product lines?

- What explains recent trends in each line?

- What is the average outgoing quality level in each product line?

- How many orders are delinquent?

- Which of the company's top twenty executives are standouts, which are low performers, and why?

- Which departments could recover from a major competitive shock, and which are vulnerable to change?

- What are the yields, costs, and cycle times at every manufacturing operation?

- What explains the company's stock market valuation relative to that of its competitors?

Curveball Questions

Answers follow—No peeking.

1. How long did the Hundred Years War last?
2. Which country makes Panama hats?
3. From which animal do we get catgut?
4. In which month do Russians celebrate the October Revolution?
5. What is a camel's-hair brush made of?
6. The Canary Islands in the Atlantic are named after what animal?
7. What was King George VI's first name?
8. What color is a purple finch?
9. Where are Chinese gooseberries from?
10. How long did the Thirty Years War last?

Answers to Curveball Questions

1. 116 years, from 1337 to 1453.

2. Ecuador.

3. From sheep and horses.

4. November. The Russian calendar was thirteen days behind ours.

5. Squirrel fur.

6. The Latin name was Insularia Canaria— "Island of the Dogs."

7. Albert. When he came to the throne in 1936, he respected the wish of Queen Victoria that no future king should ever be called Albert.

8. Distinctively crimson.

9. New Zealand.

10. Thirty years, of course—from 1618 to 1648!

Legal Considerations

The following section was written by Patricia A. Murphy, Esq., of the law firm of Otis & Hogan in San Francisco.

Did you know that...

- Many employees believe that once they are hired, they have some "right" to the job. You should check the law in your state. In some states like California, unless you and your employer agree otherwise, your employment may be "at will." This means that after you are hired, even after several years of employment, you can be terminated at any time for any reason that does not violate the law (e.g., discrimination, whistle blowing). At-will employers sometimes include at-will statements on their applications and offers of employment. They almost always have a copy in their employee handbooks. Some employers will agree to give a contract (get it in writing) stating that you can be terminated only for "good cause." The best "good cause" contracts define good cause (e.g., misconduct, conviction of a felony, gross negligence, material failure to perform the job).

- If your prospective employer is covered by the Americans with Disabilities Act or similar state law, it cannot require you to take a preemployment physical examination until after you have been offered the position. If the employer has a job-related basis for requiring a physical, it can make a job offer conditioned on your passing the physical, but it cannot require you to take the physical first. In California, the employer must pay for such an exam.

- These days, many employers will refuse to give a substantive reference to prospective employers. They will only give the title and dates of employment (and perhaps salary, if authorized by the employee). This is, of course, to avoid claims such as defamation arising out of a more detailed reference. Before you leave a job, try to get a written reference or letter of recommendation from your manager.

Try to get one of your managers to agree that prospective employers can call him or her directly for references. (Be aware that employers who have a policy of not giving substantive references will frown on this practice.)

- If you agree to perform services as an independent contractor as opposed to as an employee, you may be giving up substantial rights and benefits. For example, you will not be protected by federal and state wage-and-hour laws or covered by workers' compensation. You probably will not be entitled to employee benefits such as health insurance and pension benefits. Also, you will be responsible for paying your own taxes, since they will not be withheld from your paycheck. Know and understand all of the pros and cons before you agree to an independent contractor relationship. If you really **prefer** to be an independent contractor, get a written agreement defining the terms of the relationship. Even this may not be determinative in the end, though, because the IRS or the Department of Labor or a court may decide that, under the law, you are actually a "statutory employee" entitled to the protections and benefits of an employee. For example, "freelancers" who worked for Microsoft and signed contracts identifying them as independent contractors were later deemed employees, and Microsoft had to provide 401(k) and stock purchase plan benefits. The determination depends on many factors —principally, who has the right to control the means and manner in which your work is done, you or the employer. Where you perform the work is also a factor. *Note: As of January 1, 2000, California independent contractors are protected from harassment (but not other types of discrimination) based on race, national origin, gender, religion, and disability.*
- Federal and state equal-pay laws require that men and women receive equal pay for equal work.
- No law requires employers to give nonunion employees regular

pay increases. The only obligation an employer has to do so arises out of its contractual obligations and its own policies, which must be applied fairly and evenly.

- If you sign an agreement to arbitrate any disputes with your employers, you may be giving up your right to take any case you may have later against your employer to court, unless the agreement is found to be unfair.
- If the employer has an employee handbook, the provisions of the handbook may be binding on you as part of your employment contract. You should therefore ask to see it before you accept the job.
- Sexual harassment has become the focus of much attention and litigation recently. You should not ignore or tolerate inappropriate language, gestures, or conduct in the workplace. Note that it is not only illegal to sexually harass employees—it is also illegal to sexually harass applicants. After you are hired, you can do your part to eliminate this problem from the workplace by reporting harassment immediately if you are a victim or a witness; avoiding personal relationships at work; and always treating your co-workers (managers, peers, and subordinates) with respect.

Bottom Line

Ask questions and get answers up front. Many problems that typically arise after the working relationship begins can be avoided if all of the issues are addressed before you accept the position and start work.

More Games You Should Know About

1. **The "Not Hiring" Game:** Your job is to get in the door and make someone's life better. Every company has problems, and the question is, How can you help solve them? Never, ever, believe that companies aren't looking for talented people. They almost always are.

2. **The Application Game:** If you fail to complete an application fully and neatly, it says something about your attention to detail. Your application will suffer the same fate as if your resume had typos. Therefore, under "Employment History" don't write "See resume." It will only demonstrate your inability to follow directions and complete a task.

    While it rarely pays to be too cute on an application, creativity can serve you well. Here's the beginning of an actual application submitted by a seventeen-year-old to a McDonald's in Florida—and, yes, he was hired.

Name: Greg B.

Sex: Not yet. Still waiting for the right person.

Desired position: Company president or vice-president. But seriously, whatever's available.

Desired salary: $185,000 a year plus stock options. If that's not possible, make an offer and we can haggle.

Education: Yes.

Last position held: Target of middle-management hostility.

Do you have a car?: I think the more appropriate question here would be "Do you have a car that works?"

Do you certify that the above is true and complete to the best of your knowledge: Yes. Absolutely.

Sign here: Aries

3. **The Paper Tiger Game:** This game is played at all levels, from hourly service workers to seasoned executives who lead world-class organizations. If an interviewer schedules a short interview, they may want to be sure you—who look great on paper—look equally great in person.

    When the trustees of Stanford University were looking for a new president several years ago, they chose a search committee and narrowed their prospects down to about fifteen. The question became not only which one would be the winner, but also how to save about a dozen high-profile semifinalists the embarrassment of tossing their hats in the ring, only to be eventually rejected.

    The search committee devised a simple strategy. Not an interview exactly, but a first cousin. They visited all fifteen presidents and deans at their colleges or homes and asked what would they look for if they were members of Stanford's search committee? In this way, the fifteen acted as consultants to the search group, a strategy that garnered lots of thoughtful ideas.

    For the dozen academic leaders who didn't make the final cut, there were no embarrassing moments, no tarnished reputations, and no diplomatic rejection letters. Most of the candidates were flattered to be asked their opinion, and the committee got a good look at all of them while settling on three candidates for the final round.

4. **The Spy Game:** This is a very rare game, and it's usually played only among top executives. You should expect that an employer will check your references and your previous track record, but I know of one New Jersey firm that employed a driver to act as a spy. While driving two candidates back to New York, he listened as they talked about their interviews and then he reported back to the company.

    When a company hires someone to listen to your conversation—and "the company" isn't the CIA—consider that the interview isn't over until you step out of range. Act and speak accordingly.

5. **The "Good Old Days" Game:** Let's say that you're Generation X, Y, or Z—and the hirer is Generation A, B, or C. Consciously or unconsciously, he or she may be thinking, "Young people today want stock options. They have no loyalty. They leave good jobs, because making a life is more important than making a living."

    Most interviewers aren't this obvious, but if you suspect the interviewer is playing the "good old days" game, it may be his or her way of asking where you stand and if you plan to be around in three years. So it may help to know a few facts about the old and new days.

    In 1960, the average person had one job and one career over a working lifetime. Today, the average person at the outset of his or her working life can expect to have seven jobs and two careers.

In 1960, the average person needed to learn one new skill a year to prosper in the workplace. Today, the average person needs to learn one new skill a day.

In 1960, 23 million American women worked for pay. Today, more than 61 million do.

In 1960, the average American father spoke with his children forty-five minutes a day. Today, the average father speaks with his child six minutes a day.

If you and the interviewer are on a different page, you might mention that it's more than simply attitudes that have changed, citing some of the above examples. You might also assure the interviewer that you're as interested in the longevity of your job as he is. Other than that, the best you can do is produce results and hope (but not promise) to meet his goals, which include staying on the job.

6. **The "Rejection" Game:** Should you ever take "No" for an answer? No. If you are turned down for a job, you can always say, "I really love your company. Although I didn't get an offer, if you need someone in a few months—please keep me in mind." I know of several candidates who got to "Yes" because they refused to take "No" for an answer. They never gave in, and they won the game.

Caveat: Of course, if you have to keep begging for a job, it may be the wrong fit.

Interview Words to Remember

A survey of vice presidents and personnel directors of the nation's largest 100 corporations turned up these actual questions and comments from job candidates.

- "What are the zodiac signs of all the board members?"
- "Does your company have a policy regarding concealed weapons?"
- "At times I have a strong urge to do something harmful or shocking."
- "Sometimes I feel like smashing things."
- "I feel uneasy indoors."
- "Why aren't you in a more interesting business?"
- "Why am I here?"
- "I know this is off the subject, but will you marry me?"

The Job Hunter's Internet

Let's say you're just beginning the job search. You know where you want to live and what industry you want to work in. You should start with your network, then check out the Internet.

Most major companies feature employment sections on their Web sites that list available positions and necessary qualifications. (Cisco Systems' jobs page gets 500,000 page views a month.) You can also scan job sites such as Monster.com, which currently lists more than 200,000 job openings. And there are literally thousands of sites on which you can post a resume.

The best place to start an online job search is probably the Web page of your local college career center, which will list many more links than I could fit on these pages. However, the following sites may be helpful:

Monster.com's Monster Campus:
campus.monster.com

The Riley Guide:
www.rileyguide.com

Career Mosaic's College Connection:
www.careermosaic.com/cm/cc/cc1.html

The Entry-Level Job-Seeker Assistant:
members.aol.com/dylander/jobhome.html

The Nonprofit Career Center:
www.idealist.org/career.html

I'd also suggest checking out the following sites:

Big job databases:

www.occ.com

www.ajb.dni.us

www.careerpath.com

www.headhunter.net

For salary comparison data:

www.dbm.com/jobguide/salary.html

For insider information on working at a company:

www.vaultreports.com

www.wetfeet.com

For conducting legal research on a company:

Dun & Bradstreet

www.dnb.co.nz/

Lexis-Nexis

www.lexis.com

For conducting public records searches, I'd start with:

www.secret-subjects.com

www.gaprs.com

www.freepublicrecords.com

www.cdb.com/public/access

www.peoplewise.com

Resource Books

Career Change

Discovering Your Career in Business, Drs. Timothy Butler & James
    Waldroop (Reading, Mass.: Addison, Wesley, 1997).

Do What You Are, Paul D. Tieger and Barbara Barron-Tieger
    (New York: Little, Brown, 2nd ed. 1995).

Love Your Work and Success Will Follow, Arlene Hirsch
    (New York: John Wiley, 1996).

What Color Is Your Parachute? Richard Bolles
    (Berkeley, Calif.: Ten Speed Press, republished yearly).

Career Search

Guide to Internet Job Searching, Margaret Riley-Dickel
    (Lincolnwood, Ill.: NTC/Contemporary Publishing, 2000–1).

In Transition, Mary Lindley Burton and Richard A. Wedemeyer
    (New York: Harper Business, 1991).

The Harvard Business School Guide to Finding Your Next Job,
    Bob Gardella (Boston: Harvard Business School Press, 2000).

The Princeton Review Guide to Your Career 1999, Alan B. Bernstein and
    Nicholas R. Schaffrin (New York: Random House, 1998).

What Color Is Your Parachute? Richard Bolles
    (Berkeley, Calif.: Ten Speed Press, republished yearly).

Cover Letters

200 Letters for Job Hunters, William S. Frank
    (Berkeley, Calif.: Ten Speed Press, rev. 1993).

Dynamic Cover Letters, Katherine Hansen and Randall S. Hansen, Ph.D.
    (Berkeley, Calif.: Ten Speed Press, rev. 1995).

National Business Employment Weekly: Cover Letters, Taunie Besson
    (New York: John Wiley, 2nd ed. 1996).

The Perfect Cover Letter, Richard H. Beatty (Holbrook, Mass.: Adams
    Media, 2nd ed. 1997).

Interviewing Books

The Complete Q & A Job Interview Book, Jeffrey G. Allen
(New York: John Wiley, 2nd ed. 1997).

Knock 'Em Dead—with Great Answers to Tough Interview Questions,
Martin Yate (Holbrook, Mass.: Adams Media, republished yearly).

National Business Employment Weekly: Interviewing, Arlene S. Hirsch
(New York: John Wiley, 2nd ed. 1996).

Sweaty Palms: The Neglected Art of Interviewing, H. Anthony Medley
(Berkeley, Calif.: Ten Speed Press, rev. 1993).

Negotiating Books

Getting to Yes: Negotiating Agreement without Giving In, Roger Fisher
(New York: Penguin Books, 2nd rev. ed. 1991).

*How to Argue and Win Every Time: At Home, at Work, in Court, Everywhere,
Every Day*, Gerry Spence (New York: St. Martin's Press, 1996).

*Winning with Integrity: Getting What You're Worth Without Selling Your
Soul*, Leigh Steinberg (New York: Random House, 1998).

You Can Negotiate Anything, Herb Cohen (New York: Bantam Books, 1989).

Networking Books

Dig Your Well Before You're Thirsty, Harvey Mackay (New York Currency
Doubleday, 1997)

National Business Employment Weekly: Networking,
Douglas B. Richardson (New York: John Wiley, 1994).

*Networking for Everyone: Connecting with People for Career and Job
Success*, L. Michele Tullier (Indianapolis, Ind.: JIST Works, 1998).

Richard Beatty's Job Search Networking (Holbrook, Mass.: Adams
Media, 1994).

Writing Books

Elements of Style, William Strunk, Jr., and E. B. White (Needham
Heights, Mass.: Allyn & Bacon, 3rd ed. 1995).

On Writing Well, William K. Zinsser (New York: Harper, 6th ed. 1998).

Notes

The material in this book stems from my experiences from 1982 to 2000. Specific names and companies are used with permission. However, some stories come from the sources listed below. Where no name appears, the story is a composite, and any similarity to an actual organization or person, living or dead, is purely coincidental.

page 1　The Strengths and Weakness Charts are excerpted and adapted from the following sources: "Introduction to Type in Organizations," Sandra Krebs Hirsh & Jean Kummerow, CPP, Second edition, 1990. "Organizational Tendencies," Earle C. Page, CAPT, 1985. *Please Understand Me*, David Keirsey & Marilyn Bates, Prometheus, Third edition, 1978. *Type Talk* and *Type Talk at Work*, Otto Kroeger & Janet M. Thuesen, Delta, 1988 and 1992. And YPO University and Seminar experience with the MBTI by Pierre Mornell, 1982–1994.

page 3　"A Cautionary Tale": I received this widely distributed story via the Internet on December 18, 1998.

page 8　*Dead Poets Society:* Directed by Peter Weir, screenplay by Tom Schulman, 1989.

page 8　Pierre Mornell, *Hiring Smart*, (Berkeley, Ten Speed Press, 1998).

page 13　Michael Jordan: A series of articles in the *New York Times*, January 13 &14, 1999, pgs. A24 and C21–23.

page 15　The Jim Ansara story: Jim Ansara, personal communication, May 1999.

page 16　The Website Pros and Cons: Personal communication with two anonymous Stanford graduate students of business in March 1999.

page 18　The Levi-Strauss example: Nancy Spector, personal communication on April 12, 1999.

page 19　The Internet stories: Wetfeet.com (San Francisco: Wetfeet.com, 1998) and VaultReports.com: Kate Kaibni, personal communication May 5, 1999.

page 23　Calvin Coolidge quote: The Park Community, Inc., Park Quote #2, Internet, http://eros.thepark.com/favquote2.htm.

page 23 Networking: Adapted from Bob Gardella, the *Harvard Business School Guide to Finding Your Next Job*, (Boston: Howard Business School Press, 2000), pg. 40.

page 23 The Quad Graphics story: Nancy Ho, Quad Graphics in a personal communication on May 15, 1999.

page 24 The TravelSmith story: Our seminar was held at the Alta Mira Hotel, Sausalito, California, in 1998.

page 28 Stephanie Armour, "The New Interview Etiquette," *USA Today*, November 23, 1999, pg. B1.

page 31 Resume bloopers: Diane Stafford, "Hiring Expert Has Serious Reason for Collecting Resume Bloopers," *Marin Independent Journal*, March 22, 1992, pg. E1.

page 32 "Resumes—Top Ten List": Adapted from Gardella, see above.

page 33 Jeff Reifman story: Tina Kelley, "Making Money, Giving Money" *New York Times*, January 31, 1999, pg. BU2.

page 33 The Chris Cornyn story: Chris Cornyn, personal communication, April 1999.

page 37 "Seventy percent of candidates… ": Rayne Wolfe, "What Works," *San Francisco Examiner*, March 14, 1999, pg. J8.

page 39 The FDR story: William K. Zinsser, *On Writing Well*, (New York: Harper 6th ed. 1998), pg. 8.

Page 39 Performance Reviews: David O. Mann, personal communication on April 25, 1999.

page 45 The Danny Stern example: Danny Stern, personal communication, 1998.

page 53 The Dr. Joseph Bell story: David Walton, "Sherlock Holmes's Maker," *New York Times Book Review*, May 2, 1999, pg. 34.

page 59 The Diversity story: Historical U.S. population data (from *U.S. Statistical Abstract 1997* and *Historical Statistics of the United States: Colonial Times to 1970*, both published by the U.S. Dept. of Commerce, Bureau of the Census). Linda Mornell, Founder and Executive Director, Summer Search Foundation, personal communication on May 25, 1999.

page 66 The La Scala Opera Singer: Eileen C. Shapiro, "Author's Note," *The Seven Deadly Sins of Business*, (Oxford: Capstone Publishing, 1999).

page 68 "Be Yourself": Michelle Cottle, "Taking Charge in Interviews," *New York Times*, September 20, 1998. Machiavelli, *The Prince*, 1532.

page 69   "Talk Isn't Cheap... ": Joan E. Rigdon, "Talk Isn't Cheap," *Wall Street Journal*, February 27, 1995, pg. R3.

page 80   The Human Resources Game: Jim Ansara, Anna Finke, and Milo Shelly, personal communication, June 1999.

page 99   The Mike Shanahan story: "Head Coach," *Bronco Report*, Denverbroncos.com, pgs. 1–3.

page 99   "I fell off the horse... ": Rigdon, pg. R3.

page 107   Statistics on Lying: These come from *Hiring Smart*, and Karen Thomas, "Teen Ethics: More Cheating And Lying," and *USA Today*, October 19, 1998, pg. 1, and Erica Goode, "To Tell The Truth It's Awfully Hard To Spot A Liar," *New York Times*, May 11, 1999, pg. D1, and "Lewinsky 'Live' Won't Be Any Easier To Read," Associated Press, *San Francisco Chronicle*, February 4, 1999, pg. A13.

page 107   The Bill Ford, Jr. Story: Ira Miller, "League Criticized for Its Lack of Goodwill: Lions Official—'CIA' Has Nothing on This Place," *San Francisco Chronicle*, April 5, 1999, pg. C7.

page 110   "Do Lunch or Be Lunch": The title is from a book by the same name. Howard H. Stevenson and Jeffrey L. Cruikshank, *Do Lunch or Be Lunch*, (Boston: Harvard Business School Press, 1998).

page 114   The poison ice cube story: Marilyn Vos Savant. "Ask Marilyn," *Parade*, April 4, 1999, pg. 9. Additional trick questions in this section from "The Genius Test," *Marin Independent Journal*, March 29, 1999, pg. E1.

page 115   The ad agency trick question: Chuck Porter of Crispin, Porter & Bogusky. Personal communication, May 12, 1999.

page 130   The Gabriela Andersen-Scheiss story: Cliff Temple, "Athletics' Great Leap Forward." Games of the XXIIIrd Olympiad, Los Angeles, 1984 Commemorative Book, pg. 71.

page 131   "Anything that is completed is beautiful": Paul MacCready. Ken Carbone, Howard Schatz, Paul MacCready, *The Virtuoso*, (New York: Stewart, Tabori & Chang, 1999), pg. 67.

page 133   Accountemps statistics: Armour, pg. B1.

page 133   The Restoration Hardware story: Michael Moore, personal communication, April 18, 1999.

page 135   "The $8 Million Doorknob": *Inc*. Special 20th Anniversary Issue: 1979–1999, pg. 116.

page 140   Performance Reviews: *Fortune*, July 21, 1997, pg. 174. Also received via the Internet on April 29, 1998.

page 141   The References Top Ten List: Gardella, pg. 9.

page 145   The Siebel Systems example: Ben Balbale, personal communication, May 1999.

page 157   John Nabor: Stan Greenberg, *The Guinnes Book of Olympics Facts and Feats*, the Games, 1976, pg. 78.

pages 172–75   Forty Questions: Mornell, *Hiring Smart*, pgs. 64 & 187–190. Ten Questions: T.E. Rogers's "No-Excuse Management," *Harvard Business Review*, July-August 1990, pg. 86.

page 177   Curveball Questions: "World's Easiest Quiz?" received via Internet on August 20, 1998.

page 182   The McDonalds application story: I received this via the Internet on February 6, 2000.

page 183   The Stanford story: A Stanford trustee told me about this process several years ago.

page 185   "In 1960… ": Jim Taylor, Watts Wacker, Howard Means, the *500-Year Delta* (New York: Harper, 1998), pgs. 152–153.

page 186   Interview Words to Remember: Natasha Kassulka, "Job Applicants Can Be Weird," *Wisconsin State Journal*, March 30,1995, pg. 2.

page 187   Internet sites: Dave Murphy, Editor, Career Section, *San Francisco Examiner*, personal communication on April 16, 1999. *New York Times*, April 29, 1999, pg. D6.

Acknowledgments

I am profoundly grateful to Kirsty Melville and Aaron Wehner of Ten Speed Press and Kit Hinrichs and David Asari of Pentagram Design, who were again my peerless partners on this book. Kit also suggested Regan Dunnick, our brilliant illustrator. So special thanks to them all. I am also indebted to the many friends who took time from their busy schedules to provide insightful comments on earlier drafts of the manuscript: Robin Bacci, Connie Bagley, Jack Boland, Robin Bradford, Chris Cornyn, Chris Darwall, John Davis, Cliff Ehrlich, Caroline Little, Jeffrey Seglin, Nancy Spector, and Anthony Villanti.

In addition, I owe a debt of gratitude to Laurel Bertoncini, my secretary, who typed draft after draft after draft after draft and still kept her good humor, and to Doris Ober, who used a combination of a velvet glove and iron fist to help translate my complicated ideas into simple declarative sentences.

Special thanks also go to Jim Ansara, Patricia Murphy, Terry Ryan, Melissa Stein, and Jonathan White for their specific suggestions, and to Milo Shelly and Anna Fincke, who were kind enough to help tremendously with the Human Resource and Negotiation Strategies, plus the Summary Charts.

My family—as always—offered extremely astute comments on previous versions of the manuscript. They were very helpful.

I was mighty lucky to work with them all.

About the Author

 **Pierre Mornell** is a psychiatrist who helps presidents of companies, large and small, evaluate and select key people.

He received his BA degree from UCLA where he graduated Phi Beta Kappa and summa cum laude in English literature. He received his MD degree from UC Medical School in San Francisco, then interned at the Los Angeles County General Hospital before doing a four-year psychiatric residency at the Langley Porter Institute.

Dr. Mornell has served as an advisor to the presidents of organizations as diverse as Intuit, Kinko's, Northern Telecom (Canada), American Golf Corporation, Hellman & Friedman, Young Presidents' Organization, World Presidents' Organization, PowerBar, Pentagram, the Institute for the Future, and Art Center College of Design. He also has lectured in IBM's Advanced Management Seminar and International Executive Programs and the Harvard Business School.

Dr. Mornell was a founding director of the Trust for Public Land. He also served as a trustee of the Bolinas-Stinson Beach School Board and San Francisco University High School. Currently, he serves on the steering committee of Harvard Business School's new research center in Menlo Park, California.

He has been married for thirty-four years and has a son and two daughters. He lives in Marin County, north of San Francisco.

About the Designer

 **Kit Hinrichs** is a principal in Pentagram Design, Inc., an international design consultancy.

After graduating from the Art Center College of Design, Los Angeles, Kit worked as a graphic designer in several New York design offices. In 1965, he formed his first partnership—Russell & Hinrichs. He cofounded Jonson, Pedersen, Hinrichs, and Shakery in 1976, and became a principal in Pentagram, San Francisco, in 1986.

His accumulated design experience incorporates a wide range of projects—corporate identities, annual reports, Web sites, sales promotions, exhibits, and editorial design for clients such as AT&T, Sony, Time Warner, Monterey Bay Aquarium, Gymboree, Potlatch, Fox River Paper, Transamerica, United Airlnes, and San Jose Museum of Art.

His work is part of the permanent collection of the Museums of Modern Art (New York and San Francisco) and the Library of Congress.

About the Illustrator

Regan Dunnick is a freelance illustrator and a full-time faculty member at his alma mater, the Ringling School of Art and Design.

Regan has exhibited nationally and internationally and has won numerous medals and awards in such major exhibitions as the United Nations Environmental Show, the Hiroshima Memorial Design Show (Japan), and the American Institute of Graphic Arts exhibition. His work is in the permanent collection of the Library of Congress.

Regan's clients include *Atlantic Monthly, Playboy, Rolling Stone,* the *Washington Post,* the *New York Times, G.Q.,* and *Business Week.*

Index

Index

computer skills, when to include on a resume, 32

construction jobs, finding, 144

contingent offers, time line for, 29

control

    maintaining during interviews, 68–70

    of negotiating factors, 146

    over which interview questions are discussed, 15

conventional wisdom, 9

Cornell University, 59

Cornyn, Chris, 33

cover letters

    books about, 189

    game and strategy tip about using, 36

    guidelines for writing good, 37–38

    how to personalize, 40

    people to send copies to, 38

    reason for using, 29

    what to include in, 18, 39

curveball questions, 69, 114–117, 177–178

D

Dead Poets Society (film), 8

Decca Recording Company, 129

demographic changes in the United States, 58–59

    and the "talent war," 157

Denny's Restaurants, 58

Denver Broncos, 99

dependable personality type, 21

details, importance of attending to, 134–136

Detroit Lions, 107

dinner invitations, how to handle, 110–112

discrimination, legal protections from, 180

Distracted and Charismatic Type personality, 113

diversity and the job search, 56–61

Dodge and Cox (San Francisco investment firm), 59–60

doorknob, the $8-million, 135

drug/security tests, time line for, 29

Dun and Bradstreet, searches of, 19–20, 188

Duty, Honor, Country Type personality, 35

E

eBay, 28

e-cruiting, 28

Edinburgh Medical School, 53

eight-million dollar doorknob, the, 135

e-mail

    contacting prospective employers via, 27–28

    ensuring an e-mail back, 28–29

    game and strategy tip about using, 26

    sending thank-you notes via, 133

    using after an interview, 120

    versus voice mail as job search tool, 28

Emory, Dana, 59–60

employee evaluations

    asking for six-month instead of yearly, 148

    using quotations from one's, 39

employee handbooks, legal status of provisions in, 181

employees

    nonunion, 180–181

    statutory, 180

employers. *See* bosses; prospective employers

employment

    finding. *See* job search

    questions about why you are leaving previous, 85–86

    tryout periods, 142–145

equal pay for equal work laws, 180

Ernest & Julio Gallo Winery, 123

executive candidates, 110–112, 176, 182–183

F

faxes, sending after an interview, 120

Federal Express Corporation, 156

final interviews, time line for, 29

first impressions, 76

flexibility, importance of, 44–46

flyers, using in job search, 33–34

football teams, 99, 108

Ford, Bill Jr., 107–108

Ford Motor Company, 107

four S's for answering questions, 69

Fuller, Buckminster, 99

G

games companies play. *See also* strategies

    Application Game, 182

    asking the opposite question, 104

    "Good Old Days" Game, 184–185

    "Not Hiring" Game, 182

    Paper Tiger Game, 183

    problematic essence of the, 5

    "Rejection" Game, 185

    Spy Game, 184

    summary chart of the, 161–171

General Electric, 172

General Motors, 108

generation gaps and communication, 78

goals

    candidates' two necessary, 10

    interview questions about, 86

    of this book, 8

Goldman Sachs, 111

Greenberg, Bob, 45

gut feelings, trusting in one's, 76–78

Index

Index

public records, searches of, 109, 188
publishing companies, interviewing at, 85

Q

Quad Graphics, 23–24
questions, candidates'. *See also* interview
    questions
    sending list of after the interview, 120
    that interviewers should be asked, 118–120
    when to ask about legal issues, 181

R

Race Relations, Urban Alliance on, 58–59
racial groups in U.S. population, 58, 60
receptionists, prospective employers', 48–51
recruiting. *See* hiring process
reference checks
    strategies used by companies to obtain, 139–140
    time line for, 29
references
    availability for contacting, 139
    examples of bad, 140
    obtaining written, 179–180
    ten rules for utilizing, 141
    when to talk with one's, 138, 141
rehearsing for interviews, 70, 105
Reifman, Jeff, 33
rejection, dealing with, 185
researching prospective employers, 14–21
    finding their biases, 58
responsible personality type, 125
Restoration Hardware, 133
resume
    avoiding errors on, 31
    falsifications on, 107
    follow-up strategies after sending, 27–28
    game and strategy tip about what to include on, 30
    recommended length of, 29
    sending other materials with, 33
    sending to two places in same company, 82
    ten techniques for writing a good, 32
    using a flyer instead, 33–34
    Web sites on which you can post, 187
reviews
    asking for six-month instead of yearly, 148
    using quotations from one's, 39
Risk Taker personality type, 71

S

Saint personality type, 41
salary packages
    discussing during interviews, 86–87
    knowing what to ask for, 147
    legal considerations about, 180–181
    Web site with data on, 188
sales positions, researching, 18
San Francisco Conservatory of Music, 45
San Francisco 49ers, 99
schedule changes, 44–46
search firms, percent hired through, 25
Searles, Mickey, 99, 123–124
secretaries, prospective employers', 48–51
self-promotional flyers, 33–34
sexual harassment, 181
Shanahan, Mike, 99
Shawmut Design and Construction (Boston), 15
Shelly, Milo, 123
Siebel Systems, 145
significant others, invitations that include
    candidates', 110–112
silence during interviews, 70
solution, demonstrating you are part of the, 90
spell check, relying on computer's, 37
sports teams, 99, 107–108, 119
spouses, invitations that include candidates',
    110–112
Stanford University, 182
statistics, using in answers to interview
    questions, 103
statutory employees, 180
Stern, Danny, 45
Stern, David, 118
strategies
    about, 8
    chart with summaries of, 161–171
    Discover the Real Problems, 90–93, 166
    "Do Lunch or Be Lunch," 110–112, 168
    Do Your Homework, 14–21, 161
    Expect Changes in Interview Schedules, 44–46,
        163
    Expect Trick Questions, 114–117, 168
    Have Your Pitch Down Pat, 68–70, 165
    Know That Most Companies Have Biases,
        56–61, 164
    Master E-Mail, 26–29, 161
    Negotiate the Offer—Top Eight List, 146–148,
        171
    Network, Network, Network, 22–25, 161
    Observe the Clues in Front of You, 52–55, 164
    Pay Attention to Details, 134–136, 170
    Personalize Your Cover Letter, 36–40, 162
    Pick Your Best Strategies, 150–152, 171
    Predict the "Strengths and Weaknesses"
        Questions, 102–105, 167
    Predict the "Tell Me About Yourself" Question,
        94–96, 167

More Advance Praise for **Games Companies Play**

"I love the book and I think that if and when I apply for another job, I will use the suggestions, ideas, and strategies mentioned in it. I think it is going to be as powerful to job seekers as **Hiring Smart** was to employers.

David G. Price, Chairman, American Golf Corporation

"**Games Companies Play** should be required reading for every college senior."

Alan M. Dachs, CEO, Fremont Group, San Francisco, California

"**Games Companies Play** reads like a brilliant mystery novel. Page after page reveals a little more about career-building tactics in today's competitive marketplace. The information shared by Dr. Mornell is made all the more enjoyable because of his keen wit and great story telling ability. His humorous anecdotes are guaranteed to put a smile on your face."

Laurence B. Mindel, Chairman of the Board, Il Fornaio Corporation

"Landing a good job in today's economy is much like the famous knife fight scene in *Butch Cassidy and the Sundance Kid.* There may be no 'rules,' but if you don't know how the game is played, you'll lose for sure. Pierre Mornell has now provided an invaluable handbook on exactly how the job search game is won. It is a must read for anyone seeking employment."

T. Gary Rogers, Chairman and CEO, Dreyer's Ice Cream

"If you do nothing else prior to an interview, read **Games Companies Play** by Dr. Pierre Mornell. The insights offered are likely to spell the difference between your success and failure in the process."

Milo Shelly, Vice President, E&J Gallo Winery

"A wonderful job of leveling the playing field for aspiring job applicants. The hiring game is played by amateurs or professionals—and it's tough to be a professional when you haven't practiced a lot, which is true of most applicants. That's the group who will find this book most useful."
Bill Sahlman, Professor of Entrepreneurial Finance,
Harvard Business School

"Invaluable to the job seeker, but equally valuable to companies looking for employees. If you want a quality job that fits you, you need this book."
Lyda Hill, President, Seven Falls Company, Committee of 200

Innovative, refreshing and fun while communicating vital information about the often frustrating task of seeking the right job.
Max Messmer, Chairman and CEO, Robert Half International

"This very insightful and practical book pierces the corporate veil. Companies do play games interviewing job candidates, but Dr. Pierre Mornell is the world's expert in how to read people like a book."
John A. Davis, Senior Lecturer, Harvard Business School

"At PowerBar, we use the techniques in **Hiring Smart** to find and hire the great people we need to continue to grow and lead the growth of performance energy products. Now Pierre Mornell helps job seekers understand the inside recruiting, interviewing, and hiring approaches of today's dynamic growth companies so that they can work the system to their advantage and find and get their perfect job. I'll give a copy to my children when they enter the job market!"
Brian Maxwell, President & CEO, PowerBar, Inc.

"After his definitive text on separating the wheat from the chaff when hiring, Pierre has done it again for those seeking the best work."
Don Burr, President and co-CEO, SBS International

"**Games Companies Play** provides a compelling context for understanding the mysteries of hiring. And the book makes sense out of those mysteries, while acknowledging that they are indeed mysteries. There is no formula for good hiring, but here you will find insights, skills, and practices to be learned—and relearned."
Robert Johansen, President & CEO, the Institute for the Future

"**Games Companies Play** is a real winner."
Anton C. Garnier, President & CEO, Southwest Water Company

"This book evens up odds in the battle between the professional recruiter and the eager job seeker by giving practical strategies, listing important questions, and helping the individual to set realistic expectations. Everyone considering a job change should read this book very carefully. I just hope the people who I try to hire don't have access to it!"
Howard H. Stevenson, Sarofim-Rock Professor, Harvard Business School